With best wishes
to all at Nairn Academy
[especially the English
department!]

John Mitchell

CLASS STRUGGLE

A PROBATIONER'S DIARY

JOHN MITCHELL
Foreword by Jack McLean

Published by **POLYGON**
in association with
TIMES EDUCATIONAL SUPPLEMENT SCOTLAND

First published in Great Britain in 1986
by Polygon, 48 Pleasance, Edinburgh EH8 9TJ,
in association with Times Educational Supplement Scotland,
Hanover Street, Edinburgh.

ISBN 0 948275 25 1

Design by James Hutcheson.
Typeset by EUSPB, 48 Pleasance, Edinburgh EH8 9TJ.

Printed by Biddles Ltd., Guildford.

Acknowledgements

Grateful thanks to the myriad teachers and pupils across Scotland who contributed to this book, knowingly or otherwise.

Especial gratitude to Jim "Deep Throat" Dunbar, and to Linda and Christine, three good stringers, the last of them typist as well.

Thanks also Willis Pickard and all at TESS, Neville Moir, Pam Smith and all at Polygon; finally, thanks to Judith for general encouragement, being around, and letting me off the dishes while it was finished.

Foreword

When I started in the pedagogic profession, back in the 'Sixties, everything was different. For one thing there was a terrible shortage of teachers. For another I was unqualified. I was so unqualified I could have passed for a councillor on a Regional Education Committee. Back then they could have put a monkey in front of a class, and there were a goodly number of so-called teachers of a positively simian intellect about then: not like the "trained" teachers coming out of Colleges of Education today. But everything was different then.

The biggest difference was that, oddly enough, few of the appalling misfits who drifted into what was known as "uncertified teaching" — and my good friend, the novelist Alasdair Gray comes to mind immediately — failed in the task of transmitting culture from one generation to another, which is the especially pompous purpose, it is constantly said by educationists, of the school system. In short, the schools worked adequately enough to put any old, or young, banana in front of a class and get some result out of it all. This is by no means the case today, and it hasn't been for a very long time, as the protagonist of this almost semi-documentary novel found out.

This book is the saga of a young and naive "probationer" teacher, and I have seen a goodly number just like our hero, Morris Simpson. I have seen them come, and go, and quickly. The first two years of teaching — the probationary years — are damned-near traumatic to every young teacher now. Sometimes tragically so. I would not wish it on anyone, not even some of the beastlier visigoths I have met rioting behind a classroom desk. In common with most other dominies I darkly advise every young man or woman thinking of teaching as a career to consider some other line first. Pubs always need somebody behind a counter. "Simpy", whom you will meet in the pages of this book should have been better advised.

Morris Simpson, of course, is an improbable figure himself and it is unlikely that he would survive schools back in the good old days anyway, but I have met young entrants to teaching very like him all the same. The awful thing is that every teacher starting off today will encounter the same realities that Simpson meets. One of the realities which young Morris has to grapple with in this book is the conflict of the two year-long teachers strike. It was an inspired notion of the author to set his tragedy against the background of this educational disaster, because the teachers industrial action grew out of the mess that education in Scotland had become.

This is a tragic book, but no less tragic than the last fifteen years of Scottish education. It is a funny book too because, if you are, or have ever been, a teacher, if you didn't laugh, you'd greet. But, in the end, it is an angry book, and justifiably so, for it was the parsimony of some of those at the top in education which have fuelled this terrible testament to be written in the first place.

Jack McLean

Some of the characters in this book are fictitious. . . .

June — August 1984

It was a balmy summer's day in June, 1984, when Morris Simpson graduated from Jordanhill College of Education, armed with a certificate which allowed him to practise the teaching of English in the secondary schools of Scotland. Always a keen student, Morris had enjoyed his time at Jordanhill but was anxious to join the real world of wage-earners; it was, after all, five years now since he had left school and he felt ready to embark upon a career which had, he reflected, been earmarked especially for him. Two months hence, he would enter a probationary period of two years, after which time he would — in the normal course of events — be granted full registration with the General Teaching Council for Scotland.

Teaching was something of a vocation to Morris Simpson. The staffroom cynics he had encountered during his three blocks of teaching practice had done little to dent a long cherished notion that his was a gift, an offering, a fervent desire to impart knowledge unto Youth. All of his life he had wanted to teach, and the beginning of Session '84/'85 was to be the moment of truth.

Almost coincident with his graduation, however, the country's largest teaching union, the *Educational Institute of Scotland*, was holding its Annual General Meeting across the Firth of Clyde, at Rothesay. Before the ink had quite dried on Morris Simpson's final examination paper, the first salvo of warning shots had been fired in what was set to become the fiercest battle to engulf Scottish education since the heady days of Lord Houghton's pay review in 1975.

At the beginning of July, news broke in the Scottish press that teachers were set firm on a course of increasingly stringent industrial action which would commence with a refusal to undertake extra-curricular work and which would extend, in October and November, to a withdrawal from all curricular development in connection with the new Standard Grade examinations, inspired by the Munn and Dunning Reports of the 1970's, and due to be introduced in Session '85/'86.

A national strike had been recently averted — but only just. Teachers' salaries, it was felt, had fallen dramatically in real terms, so that an Honours Graduate (such as Morris) now found himself £3500 per annum behind average earnings in the country. A novice policeman, it was widely reported, would take home more in his weekly wage packet than a teacher whose five years of training might have led him to expect greater things.

Few disputed, then, the validity of the teachers' request for an independent pay review within the next six months; few quarrelled with John Pollock's* assertion that "every parent and every concerned citizen should be totally on the side of the teachers"; many recalled Lord Houghton's proclamation that "after the family, the teacher is the most important influence on the next generation." In short, few doubted that the then Secretary of State for Scotland, Mr George Younger, could reasonably refuse such a request.

It would all be over by Christmas.

For Morris Simpson, however, such warbeats were merely the brave sound of a distant drum. More immediate concerns impressed upon his young mind: when would he hear of his first appointment? Would he like his new Head of Department? Would he have a 'Higher' class to teach? How could he make a name for himself in Education? As a member of the non-striking *Professional Association of Teachers*, how would he be viewed by his more militant colleagues in the *EIS* or the *SSTA*?*

By August, though, it didn't seem as if any of this would matter, for he had still to hear from his Regional Authority's Staffing Department. Admittedly, only three out of his 42 former colleagues at Jordanhill had received any kind of posting by then, but Morris had expected swifter action, particularly when he recalled his end-of-term interview at college. . . .

"Ah . . . Morris Simpson?" the Man from the Education Authority had enquired of him across the desk. ,

"Yes, sir," Morris replied promptly, glad of his sports jacket among a student host of living, breathing denim. They could see he meant business.

*John Pollock: General Secretary of the EIS, "Scotland's largest teaching union".

* Scottish Secondary Teachers' Association: a traditionally moderate union, whose membership is restricted to Secondary Teachers.

"You've put down for Freeman Secondary, Morris. That was where you spent your second block of teaching practice, wasn't it?"

Yes, Mr . . . ?"

"Jackson."

"Yes, Mr Jackson. It's a school where I feel I'd be happy to teach."

"Oh?" Mr Jackson enquired, eyebrows raised. "And why's that?"

"I always felt *part* of the school. They had a tremendously effective student liaison scheme whereby I could actually discuss any problems which arose with a member of the school management team. And as well as that, their methods of *teaching* were so in keeping with my own views on the subject — you know, open plan classrooms, group teaching across the curriculum, pupil counselling services, block timetabling and, most importantly, a firm adherence to the inalienable rights of the child above all else."

"I see. So it's not the uniforms, then?"

Morris looked blankly across the desk. "Pardon?"

"It's not the uniforms, then? You know — the girls. Their uniforms. I've always liked that school too. They all wear uniforms there . . . " Jackson looked distracted, his gaze hovering in the middle distance. "Very sweet. Very smart, those uniforms . . . ," his voice trailed quietly into solitary reflection.

"Anyway, Simpson," he snapped into life again, "I'll see what we can do. It's — um- quite handy for your home too, isn't it?"

"Yes, Mr Jackson. I can't pretend that my travelling costs didn't come into consideration as well," confessed Morris, "but I really *do* feel that the school's educational ethos coincides so precisely with my own that it would be silly to look elsewhere at present."

"Indeed, indeed, Simpson. Well, I don't think there should be any problem. After all, it's not *every* student who walks out of here with an A Band Certificate for Teaching Practice and a merit in Professional Subjects. You should be hearing from us before very long."

Strangely enough, that was actually the *last* Morris heard from his prospective employers. Until, that is, Monday 13th August, two days before the new session was due to start. At

11

4.15 pm on that day, he received a telephone call from his Region's Staffing Department, asking him to report for duty at Parkland High School on Wednesday morning. A contract would be posted for his immediate signature.

Glad of any employment, Morris clutched delightedly at this opportunity to enter his chosen profession, but could not help pondering Mr Jackson's unfulfilled assurances. His puzzlement turned to dismay upon learning of the 55 minute bus journey to be undertaken each morning in order to reach his place of work, and he found it hard to contain his amazement when he learned of Elaine McReadie's apppointment: another first-year probationer in English, she had *asked* for a job in Parkland High but had been heard to question the sanity of Staffing Departments who forced her into a 55 minute bus journey from her home in Parkland Circus when she could have been teaching in a school on her own doorstep.

Morris, however, shelved his doubts and counted his blessings, putting his trust in the Staffing Department and averting his worries about the traditional approaches for which his new school was renowned. He was a man with implacable faith in an Educational Divinity which, he believed, was shaping his ends in the manner it best saw fit. His was not to question why, and he looked forward to the three in-service days provided by the authorities in order that curriculum development and arrangements for the new term could be effectively set in motion. As a young child waits eagerly for Christmas, so Morris waited eagerly for Wednesday. . . .

* * * * * * * * *

It was at this point that the *Times Educational Supplement Scotland* devised the notion of recording the thoughts of a typical teacher entering his first year of probationary service. Morris was approached by a representative and agreed to submit occasional extracts from events in the everyday life of such a teacher, on the understandable condition that these extracts remain anonymous.

His identity having long since been apparent, however, and his future in education being no longer in doubt, he has agreed to the publication of his diary in this more durable form. It is reproduced with the permission of the *TESS* and thereby forms a permanent record which will be, one hopes, of inestimable value to future generations of young teachers and old, as well as of general interest to a wider public seeking awareness of the tensions — and rewards — to be encountered by the novice master at the gateway of his career.

> *"Delightful task! to rear the tender thought*
> *To teach the young idea how to shoot."*

Wednesday 15th August — First In-Service Day

Well, this has been my first day as a member of the teaching profession. It's been quite exciting really, though I didn't see any pupils. I met a lot of my new colleagues, of course, and they all seem very pleasant, if slightly dejected. One chap in particular was greeting everybody with a funereal-style handshake while shaking his head sadly and saying "Commiserations" to one and all.

Most of the day was spent not actually doing very much. The headmaster gave us a lot of information sheets which he then read through with us. Maybe some of the staff can't see very well. He was also at great pains to stress that the staffroom tea-urn should henceforth be switched off between intervals and lunch-time: apparently, it had burnt out three elements last year, and he spent twenty-five minutes explaining why the education authorities were no longer prepared to provide replacements. I must say, I'd expected to be discussing more important things than tea-urns on my first day of teaching!

Anyway, I took careful notes of all the other things he said. Nobody else seemed to do this, but I always think it's wise to get a written copy of everything in case it's important. Mind you, everybody did start writing at one point just after the headmaster announced he'd received a letter on "Teachers' premature retirement".

Lots of people suddenly started scribbling on notepads and looked very alert. I didn't bother taking any notes here as I didn't think it applied to me. One young chap sitting along the bench couldn't have been more than about 30 but he was writing furiously.

I asked him laughingly, later on, if he was thinking of retiring. He just turned and fixed me with a kind of vacant stare, then muttered something about double glazing. I wonder what he meant?

Anyway, even if nothing much happened today, it's good to be a member of the teaching profession at last, after five years' hard training.

Thursday 16th August — Second In-Service Day

Met a chap called Pringle today. He asked me if I wanted to join his union, which he said was the main teachers' union in Scotland. I told him I would think about it and asked him about the young fellow I'd spoken to yesterday. He said that must have been Dickson, who'd been looking for all kinds of jobs outside teaching, the latest idea having been to become a sales representative for a double glazing company.

I said I thought it was a bit sad if someone as young as he obviously is wants to leave teaching to do *that* kind of work, which is not really the same type of profession as teaching. He just snorted and walked away after telling me I would "soon learn".

In the afternoon I met a man called Major. He asked me if I wanted to join *his* union, which he said was cheaper to join than Mr Pringle's and which would cater more for my interests as a teacher in a secondary school. I told him I would think about it too.

What I haven't told either of them yet is that I'm already *in* a union! There was a very nice fellow who came round at teacher training college and gave me "special terms" to join *his* union. What I like most about it is that his union refuse to go on strike.

I must say that I agree with that: if we are to set an example to young people we can't really go refusing to teach them just because we're getting slightly less money than some of us think we need. That would be demeaning.

I think I'll wait until our union representative calls a meeting and then just go along to that. Pringle and Major should get the message then.

Friday 17th August — Third In-Service Day

Quite an exciting day today. I've been given my timetable for the incoming sesion by my head of department (an awfully nice lady called Miss Bowman) and have been planning some lessons for next week. More of which later.

Also, the department has been busy developing some of the new courses for this session and next. Well, some of them have, at any rate. I've discovered that Messrs Pringle and Major are in the English department too, and both of them have refused to have much to do with helping the head of department in making up these new courses.

Personally, I think it's a bit much — they say they're merely complying with union instructions but it means Miss Bowman and the rest of the department have to do a lot of extra work while Pringle and Major get on with cleaning out their rooms (which I must say, are badly needing it!).

Talking of rooms, the deputy head came up to me today and apologised because the room I'd been promised has had to be re-allocated as a television room. This means that I will have to be peripatetic.

I pretended to mishear him and asked, "Did you say 'Very pathetic'?" But I don't think he realised it was a joke because he said: "No — peripatetic. That means you'll have to move around from room to room. Sorry about it but we've got to have a television room for the new courses. Lots of audio-visual stuff in them, you know."

Well, of course, I'm as keen as anybody (if not keener) on increasing the availability of educational technology (we had a course on it at college) so I readily agreed.

My timetable looks very exciting. I've got two first-year classes, one second-year class, the fifth section in third year and the bottom section in fourth year.

I think it should be very challenging. I'm going to do *Lord of the Flies* with the fourth year: got a copy from the bookstore today so will read it over at the weekend to remind myself of its allegorical content. (Better get a set of notes!)

Looking forward to next week enormously, when I actually get the chance to meet my charges for the coming year.

The Weekend

As Morris prepared for his first full week of teaching, the world at large had other concerns on its mind. A national coal strike entered its 23rd week, picket line confrontations intensified, and the second potential dock strike of that summer seemed imminent. Local authorities introduced savage restrictions on water consumption as reservoir supplies exhausted themselves and a nationwide drought became reality.

The distribution, then, of an *EIS* 'Action Pack' comprising car stickers, staffroom posters and badges, all designed to sway the public conscience, understandably engendered little excitement except in the staffrooms themselves.

To Morris, such public manifestations of discontent were unseemly anyway. The weekend held other challenges, other concerns, chief amongst which was the devising of lesson plans for those first important weeks when he had to carve an identity for himself. He was somewhat concerned to discover that his 'team teaching' colleague was to be Mr Major, towards whom he felt a certain antipathy already.

However, most of that weekend was spent in preparation for a dramatic improvisation he planned to use as an introduction to *Lord of the Flies*. This scheme involved staging a spontaneous class play with his bottom 4th Year Group by asking them to imagine the classroom as a desert island bereft of adults to supervise their activities. Thereafter, "free improvisation" was to be allowed. He conveniently dismissed chaotic memories of the one previous occasion he had used this lesson plan during teaching practice; after all, he now had the additional authority of being the *real* teacher in charge of the class, and that would surely induce sufficient respect in the children.

Sadly, none of it was to be. . . .

Monday 20th August

Well, that's my first day over, and an exciting one it's been too. The morning was taken up with obtaining registration details from my form class. They are a nice bunch of first year kids — all very nervous with smart uniforms and polished faces.

I thought it better to be straight with them and explained that I was new too and it would take us all some time to learn the geography of the school. By the end of the morning I'd discovered how true my own words were — it was very nice of the fifth year boys to redirect me to the staffroom but I'm sure I found it much more quickly last week.

I met the bottom fourth year this afternoon but had to change my plans somewhat. Having spent all weekend mugging up on *Lord of the Flies* I got to the bookstore to discover that Pringle had taken all the copies for his fifth year! I tried reasoning with him but he claimed seniority and that was that. Going to try *Animal Farm* instead.

Tuesday 21st August

An extremely hectic day. Met my second year class this morning, who turned out to be rather difficult. Fortunately, I'm involved in 'team teaching' with 2C which means the strain is somewhat less. Mr Major and I have worked out a "plan of campaign", whereby I will normally provide the "input" for the lessons and then we will both circulate, lending assistance wherever it is needed. We're going to work out a scheme to share the marking of jotters.

The third year all complained about their class reader. They say it's boring. I thought it rather unfair of them to prejudge it like that after only one chapter but I decided to be democratic and we took a vote on it. Sixteen of them wanted to do another book and 12 of them wanted to keep on with this one so I've split them into two groups and will give the 16 moaners the choice of another novel.

On top of all these difficulties I found myself in a tricky situation at lunchtime. Mr Pringle and Mr Major had called a joint meeting of both their unions to discuss some kind of pay claim and obviously, as a member of neither union, I was unable to go. In fact, it seemed I was about the only person not there and it did get rather lonely in the staffroom.

In addition to this, the deputy head had asked me to "Look after the lunch-duty for a short time" while everyone was away at the union meetings. Well, my duty day is supposed to be

Thursday, but I felt I couldn't really refuse; however, things got rather hectic after the first 40 minutes and I had to send for reinforcements after some of the first year boys were forced to perform an impromptu concert on the dining tables by some of the fifth years.

Mr Pringle came and, I thought, treated some of the fifth year boys rather harshly, but things quietened down after that. The deputy head seemed rather annoyed but I'm sure he realises that I can hardly be expected to accept responsibility for what was really only high spirited excitement at the beginning of the session.

Feel completely drained tonight, possibly as a consequence of my somewhat lengthy search to locate Class 1Q, who were in Block 1, Room 4, as opposed to Block 4, Room 1, as indicated by my timetable. Must check for further errors with the deputy head.

Wednesday 22nd August

I can't believe it. Five days into my new career and I've had to take a day off!

Woke up with a thumping head and streaming nose. Perhaps the rainstorm during my peregrinations between Blocks 1 and 4 had something to do with it.

Never mind. I'll be back tomorrow.

Thursday 23rd August

Oh God. Much worse.
I shall return tomorrow.

Friday 24th August

Staggered in this morning and met the deputy head at the front door. He stared at me rather frostily and said something about "please-takes" but I'm not quite sure what he meant.

Got the fourth year started on *Animal Farm* this morning. They said they didn't want to read a stupid baby book about farms but I soon explained to them that there was much more significance to it than that. We eventually settled down to reading it and they actually seemed to enjoy it.

They particularly liked the opening page's description of old

Major, the prize Middle White boar, and laughed a lot when he was introduced to the story. Secretly, I thought it quite an amusing coincidence that this figure should bear the same name as my departmental colleague, but I don't think these pupils would be quick enough to make that sort of connection. They are, after all, under-achievers.

One piece of important news today, among all the flurry of teaching activity: I'd been wondering all this week when our union representative would make himself known to me and, amazingly enough, I received a letter this afternoon which asked whether yours truly would be prepared to take on the position of union representative within our school

This is quite an honour. I wonder why they've selected me for the job? Perhaps it's because I made my views on striking very clear.

Anyway, it will add to my work-load somewhat, but I shall call a meeting of all our union members at the earliest opportunity next week.

Cold still with me, but I shall rest over the weekend and return, refreshed, to the fray next week.

August — September 1984

Unfortunately, Morris had displayed devotion above and beyond the call of duty by staggering into work that Friday morning, for it soon became apparent that his recovery was far from complete. A further week's absence did nothing to endear him to Mr Tod, the Deputy Head, or, indeed, to his colleagues who were in receipt of the little slips of paper which requested them to "please take Mr Simpson's class at Period 3 . . . "* In fact, according to figures released during Session '84/'85, the sudden abolition of corporal punishment in most Scottish schools, as well as a host of other stress-related problems, led to a dramatic rise in staff absenteeism, and cover for absent colleagues became a vexatious issue.

Meanwhile, propped up in bed and surrounded by class registers and lesson plans, Morris was digusted to learn of the increasing industrial unrest in Strathclyde schools. Although Parkland High was not directly affected, it was plain to him that the more militant scions of the *EIS* were simply acting out of malicious spite directed towards a Government doing its best to halt the unceasing spirals of public spending.

The Glasgow *Evening Times*, for example, had to report, on Tuesday 21st August, that there was "chaos in the classroom as Lanarkshire pupils were sent home after a walk-out by teachers over 'consortium arrangements'." This 'grouping' of local schools in an effort to use teachers more efficiently meant that subjects for which there were only small numbers of candidates in each school would be taught in one school only. From a 'consortium' of three or four schools, pupils would be 'bussed' between their 'base' school and the school wherein their chosen subject was to be taught.

Admittedly, this meant a standardisation of timetabling plans

*The derivation of the term "a please-take" is obvious from the text; in some parts of Scotland, the term "Yufti" is a more popular alternative for these sudden calls to the breach, as in the injunction, often pupil-delivered: "Yufti take Mr Gob's class at Period 3 . . . "

between local schools — not always an easy matter to arrange — and problems *did* arise in the case of the island High School of Arran, a forty-five minute ferry journey from its consortium neighbours in Saltcoats and Ardrossan; admittedly, the plan *did* seem to have been pushed through with what amounted to indecent haste and, to a profession already straining under the weights of curricular development, the dictatorial tone of instructions from a remote educational hierarchy bore all the tact of a stampeding elephant herd. The flame which lit the metaphorical touchpaper, in this case, was a letter from Edward Miller, Strathclyde's Director of Education, informing that pay would be docked from teachers who "refused to take classes of more than 25, accept changes in school timetabling, or accept pupils from other schools under new consortium arrangements connected with the 16-18 Action Plan."

On Wednesday August 22nd, more "classroom chaos" was reported by the *Evening Times*, as 6000 pupils were sent home and, on the subsequent day, when the numbers had swelled to 8000, the overburdened sub-editors were moved to proclaim — in a further startling feat of alliterative ingenuity — that "Class Chaos (was) Growing!" Malcolm Green, Chairman of Strathclyde's education committee, and an otherwise useful ally to the teachers' cause throughout their pay campaign, was moved to describe their arguments on this occasion as being "hypocritical and fallacious". Perhaps he was right, but the strength of feeling generated by these skirmishes, preludes to the real battle, served warning of the strife to come. . . .

Some of the more naive members of the profession expected such evident bitterness to result in a prompt response to the eight-week old request for an independent pay review, but George Younger still appeared unwilling to make such a commitment. In any case, there were other matters which tended to monopolise the Government's attention still: as the miners' strike entered its 24th week, the National Coal Board proudly announced, on August 27th, that 139 miners had already returned to work in Scotland, but the ever growing threat of a national dock strike persuaded the Prime Minister, Margaret Thatcher, to call "Cabinet Crisis Talks", a crisis compounded by the T.U.C. announcement, three days later, that it was prepared to back Arthur Scargill and his demands to oppose pit closures.

With the exception of inconvenienced parents, then, the teachers' tantrums were of little consequence to the world at large.

To Morris, of course, the most disgraceful aspect of the whole sorry state of affairs was the lowering respect for the profession which must ultimately result from such betrayals of integrity and dignity. Thermometer in mouth, he mentally congratulated himself upon joining a non-striking union and concentrated his attention upon the practicalities of arranging lesson plans for those occasions when he was due to 'team-teach' with Mr Major. Co-operative teaching, as it was also known, had been a particular interest of his ever since he had undertaken a college elective course for teaching strategies aimed at slow-learners. The educational benefits were obvious: particularly ineducable children could be granted individual remediation by one teacher whilst the other was involved in stretching the 'high-fliers', an essential prerequisite of effective mixed-ability teaching; more structured assessment situations could be generated when *two* teachers were present, and the reactional interfaces between children and staff were *bound* to be lessened. The lecturers at college *had* warned about the possible abuses of the system, of course, and Morris was keen to ensure that both he *and* Mr Major took a full and equal share in responding to the exciting challenges offered by Class 2C. . . .

Morris returned to work, then, on Monday August 27th, and his fears over Mr Major's contributions to co-operative teaching were, sadly, soon realised. Understandably reluctant to make criticisms of a well established member of the department, however, he buckled down to ensuring that his own commitments were honoured. Like Caesar's wife, he wished to remain above suspicion, and the late summer evenings saw him bent over increasingly awesome mountains of jotters, red pen clutched firmly in his grasp, and eyes straining to decipher the illegible scrawlings of his young charges.

Matters came to a head, however, during the week beginning September 24th, as the following extract from Morris's diary makes plain. The observant reader will notice, too, that Parkland High School had, by September, come to make its own protest over consortium schools and the Action Plan; never in the vanguard of union activism, it was nevertheless a school which aimed to ensure that its staff neither gave, nor asked for, any quarter in the pedantic intricacies of adherence to contract.

A meeting was called.

Monday September 24th

A big disagreement this morning over timetable arrangements for the senior classes! It doesn't really affect me because my most "senior" class is the bottom fourth year, but a lot of the staff are up in arms over the fact that they have to see many of their pupils for "double" periods in the afternoon.

We held a meeting at lunch-time to discuss it and all three unions were represented, including my own. Everyone seemed very worked up because they recalled that, when our school changed from 40-minute periods to 65-minute periods last session, one of the "sound educational arguments" behind the change was that pupils found a double period of one hour and twenty minutes too long to ensure continued concentration.

Now, because of something they call "consortium arrangements", it appears that some of my colleagues in, for example, the Science or History departments have to teach the same pupils for blocks of two hours and ten minutes!

I must say I don't know what they're moaning about. These new arrangements have ensured that pupils have a much wider choice of subject. There were a lot of complaints to the effect that our pupils, in fact, have a much *smaller* range of subjects from which they can choose because of the consortium, but I am convinced that such arguments are simply hypocritical and fallacious.

Tuesday 25th September

I am getting rather worried about the team-teaching arrangements between Mr Major and myself. At the beginning of the session we worked out a scheme to share the marking of 2C's jotters, but there seems to be a gross inequality of labour at present.

To date, I have marked two sets of (30) compositions, three sets of interpretation exercises and one set of literature essays. Mr Major has marked one (multiple choice) listening test. He claimed that, as this test was a model for future assessment formats in English, he (being the senior teacher) had better make sure it was "done properly" (sic!). Must have a word with Miss Bowman, my head of department.

Wednesday 26th September

I have never been so infuriated in my entire teaching career as I was today. The morning began badly enough when I overheard two members of my second year class on the stairs. One was a new girl who arrived last week and who was being asked by her friend what she thought of her new school.

"Well," she replied, "it's not bad and some of the teachers are really quite good."

"Yes," agreed the other, "but it's a pity we've got Simpy for English. (This, I believe, is a nickname for me.) He's not very good, is he? That's why he's got to have old Major with him — to help keep an eye on us and check he doesn't make a cock-up of anything."

Overlooking the flagrant disrespect of such language, I was shocked that this girl could possibly fail to realize that, as I am her class teacher, Mr Major is merely *assisting* me and that the reason for his appearance in the classroom is due to the fact that 2C has a larger proportion of under-achievers than is the norm.

If such was not evident to her this morning, then it certainly should have been by the afternoon!

Having divided 2C into six groups of five at the beginning of period four, I awaited the arrival of my elderly colleague with no little impatience. I had, after all, spent much of the previous evening preparing a lesson on group drama, an entertaining enough diversion, but one which necessitates — absolutely — the presence of more than one teacher to ensure a controlled and dignified approach to the subject.

Ten minutes after the class had arrived I decided to locate him myself. I set each group a number of improvised drama tasks and hurried along to the staffroom. What should I find but the lazy old devil with his feet up on the table, reading a paper and smoking a pipe! My wrath knew no bounds and, for a moment, I forgot myself.

"Mr Major!", I demanded. "May I remind you that *we* have a class to teach?"

"Sorry, old boy," he oozed. "Is that the time? Had to take the

24

car down to the garage over the lunch-hour to get a side-light fixed. Didn't have time for a coffee so I'm just catching up."

I glowered hard, not trusting myself to speak.

"Little blighters in, then?" he asked. "Better get along there, hadn't we?"

We returned to witness Maxwell, a thoroughly disagreeable little boy, emulating some of his heroes on *Grange Hill* (a perfectly awful television programme purporting to look at life in schools) by pinning his best friend to the floor and thrusting a knee into his pelvic area. I separated the individuals and demanded an explanation.

They claimed to be improvising a "Conflict Situation", as instructed by me, but I told them that I had dealt with more than enough conflict for one day (a subtle reference which was probably beyond Major's powers of interpretation) and issued two punishment referral sheets immediately. They did not seem unduly concerned.

Will definitely speak to Miss B about Major.

Thursday 27th September

A feather in my cap today. The headmaster called me down at the morning interval to offer me the chance of taking the fourth year football team to an away match this afternoon.

He said that the previous "coach" of the team (Mr Pickup of Geography) had decided to stand down in favour of "young blood" as he put it.

The head kindly excused me from teaching during the last period today so that I could get an "early start" with the boys at 3pm. He probably didn't realise that I already *have* a free period at this time, which I'd been going to use for correcting 2C's jotters.

Dickson, the mod langs fellow who's looking for a job as a double glazing salesman, congratulated me on the honour and said it would probably be worth a couple of Brownie points in the promotion stakes, whatever that means.

Friday 28th September

A rather unpleasant interview with the head first thing. Apparently he'd been on the 'phone to Mr McKean, his counterpart at St Ainsley's, our opponents in yesterday's match.

I pointed out that the terms of his original request had merely indicated that I should *accompany* the football team yesterday and had made no mention whatsoever of refereeing the ruddy game.

He was most displeased with my intemperate language but I felt constrained to explain, in full, that I am *not* sufficiently acquainted with the rules of Association Football to preside as arbiter in matters of dubious off-side decisions and that far less am I acquainted with the rules of professional wrestling, which knowledge might have served me well during the disgraceful scenes which followed our team's last-minute equalizer.

We parted on stormy terms but I think he will have admired me for speaking my mind.

Other members of staff didn't seem so sure, however, and I am left to ponder Dickson's words at 4pm this evening. He reminded me of what he had said about Brownie points yesterday and then walked out of the staff-room door, advising me "not to try for any badges this year".

It's all very depressing.

September — November 1984

Even more depressing, to the Scottish Education Department at any rate, was September's announcement that the *EIS* intended to withdraw from the Consultative Committee on the Curriculum and would recommend its members to refrain from *any* involvement in Standard Grade Working Parties. Allan Stewart, the hitherto invisible Scottish Education Minister, was now moved to remark that he would have to give "most careful consideration " to the teachers' case, a clearly perceived shift of tone from his Department's cursory summer response to the *SSTA*-originated request for an independent pay review.

The *EIS* move to halt Standard Grade in its tracks would, everybody knew, force Mr Younger's hand: on October 5th, the *TESS* confidently predicted a resolution to Mr Younger's deliberations — an announcement would be made "within the next few weeks".

Never one to be accused of pre-emptive action, however, the Secretary of State decided to investigate further by offering salary talks to the teachers' side of the Scottish Joint Negotiating Committee (*SJNC*), his main purpose being to ensure that he had "fully understood the case being made by the teachers and to provide an opportunity for them to bring to his attention any further points . . . relevant to his consideration of their request."

Leaders of the main teaching unions — and even one from Morris's union, the *PAT* — scurried Londonwards on October 23rd, there to frame a case. A reportedly constructive meeting ensued: Mr Younger had already studied the *SJNC* management's support for the beleagured profession and was perhaps tempted by the unions' offers to resolve the matter quickly and efficiently, thereby earning *himself* no small number of Brownie Points, as Mr Dickson would have it. Understandably, however, he felt that such an effective resolution of the affair, and its inevitable concession to an independent pay review, would have involved appending his signature to a large and very blank cheque: no amount of Brownie Badges could have compensated for the Prime

27

Ministerial wrath likely to befall him should such a cheque have been issued, so a stalemate seemed inevitable.

Indeed, the terms of his press release after the meeting — no doubt prepared long in advance — indicated a hardening of attitudes, for he deplored therein "the betrayal of trust of parents and pupils who had been offered the new courses and the threat of denying opportunities to pupils of more modest abilities". . . .

The arrows aimed at Standard Grade had found their mark.

The hustling and bustling of this week certainly meant one thing: the response could not be much longer in coming. Four long months had elapsed since those first soundings had been taken, and George Younger must surely be ready, it was thought, to make up his mind. The *TESS* of November 2nd felt confident enough — again — to let readers know that the cabinet "would be informed of his decision within the next few days" and that a Parliamentary announcement would follow soon thereafter.

Mr Younger's confidence in the continuation of Standard Grade at this point hinted broadly to many that perhaps he was actually considering a "yes" after all, for few schools possessed material for Standard Grade Courses after Christmas, and the Scottish Examination Board would hardly recommend — even in the guarded terms they used — the continuation of 'S Grade' Phases 2 and 3 if *they* didn't have an ear to the ground of Government rumblings, would they?

Nevertheless, this ostrich-like optimism remained unconfirmed by November 9th, when the *TESS* reported that Mr Younger was *still* prevaricating and began instead to ponder with what linguistic athletics he was likely to disguise his "no". But within another week the pendulum of anticipation had swung once more, so that even John Pollock had fallen prey to the optimism of earlier days: "the fact that the Secretary of State is taking so long," he claimed hopefully, "must mean that he is giving our case serious consideration. If he was just preparing to give us a stark 'no' he would have done so this week when there was plenty of bad news for him to hide under."

Indeed there was. The bi-annual threat to sever the jugular vein of Scotland's steel industry at Ravenscraig had just been announced, the miners had dangled a noose, literally, over the head of Norman Willis, TUC General Secretary, because he had the temerity to condemn picket-line violence, and Education Secretary Sir Keith Joseph was scoring one of his most spectacular own goals that year by proposing to claw back large slices of grant money from student-encumbered parents — and alienating large percentages of middle-class Tory support in the process. A refusal to allocate more money to Scottish teachers would have merited but little media attention that week — yet still they waited.

Working in best Scout traditions, the *EIS* prepared itself for action in the event of a negative decision by Mr Younger, and the likelihood of strikes by Christmas loomed large. Pockets of resistance had already broken out through the months of October and November, anyway: in Glasgow and Lanarkshire, amongst other Divisions, further walk-outs had occurred over the still controversial matter of cover for absent colleagues. Most teachers were ready for a fight.

Even Mr Major's union, the *SSTA*, found itself involved in a ballot of members regarding their willingness to take further industrial action over extra-contractual responsibilities such as supervision of school lunches and corridor duty during intervals, as well as the more publicised unwillingness to participate in the development of Standard Grade Examinations.

It was little surprise that young men such as Alan Dickson wanted to leave teaching for the relatively peaceful — and certainly more remunerative — shores of double glazing sales, and it was small surprise that Morris Simpson found little time to transmit his thoughts to paper through the torrid weeks of October. By the end of November, however, he was coming more closely to terms with his teaching duties and found space to record the disturbing divisions which had emerged within Parkland High as a result of the dispute.

Monday 26th November

Quite a fuss today over corridor duty and lunchtime supervision: apparently both Mr Major and Mr Pringle have complied with their respective unions' instructions and ordered that all such extra-contractual activities be suspended forthwith.

They are calling it "industrial action" but that seems a

peculiar misnomer to me and I can't help but observe that their attitude will inevitably affect the discipline within the school.

As a member of a non-striking union I have decided to make a stand: I spoke to the depute head this morning and offered to help out with any of the duties which my more militant colleagues have seen fit to abandon. He seemed very pleased to accept my offer and immediately added my name to the newly-devised rota on his study wall.

I am to share lunch-time supervision with the headmaster on Mondays and Thursdays as well as assisting the depute himself on Tuesdays and Fridays. Interval corridor duty will be my "special remit", however: the depute asked me to circulate other staff and "sound them out" by emphasising the need for co-operation and the fact that their action was likely to have little effect upon the education authorities; on the contrary, he claimed, the only people to be inconvenienced would be himself and the headmaster.

Why, then, he continued, could they not "find it within themselves to lend a hand in this time of need?"

I must say I agree with him and so I expressed my willingness to locate a sympathetic ear or two. He *did* warn me that this might be "rather a sensitive area" but I don't really think that responsible adults are likely to object when a simple request such as this is made to them.

We shall see. . . .

Tuesday 27th November

A mysterious and alarming incident this morning. Having entered the corridor leading to my room, I could not help but observe the somewhat furtive figure of Mr Pringle emerging around the corner of my door, casting wary glances to left and to right.

"Morning, Mr Pringle!" I boomed down the passage, whereupon he jumped in the air like a scalded cat!

"Oh! Um . . . Hello . . . er . . . Mr . . . ah . . . Simpson," he stuttered. "Didn't . . . eh . . . hear you coming there. . . ."

"Semper vigilans," I smiled, edging past him with a briefcase full of corrected jotters.

"Just . . . er . . . looking for a few spare copies of *Animal Farm*," he interjected, seeming to regain his equilibrium. I had

30

just offered to locate the said books on his behalf when I glanced in the direction of my blackboard. There, in chalked letters 3ft high, was the outrageous inscription "SIMPY IS A SCAB!"

Well, of course I was beside myself with rage. To think that secondary school pupils should sink to such depths! Pringle, for all our differences in the past, seemed to feel every sympathy for me: he stood shaking his head in disbelief before giving me a consolatory pat on the shoulder and walking out of the room.

Wednesday 28th November — am

I am launching an attempt to locate the instigators of the "blackboard incident". As Wednesday is my "day off" for lunch duties I sought out Pringle and broached my latest theory concerning the matter. I recalled a recent conversation with my bottom fourth year wherein we discussed the possibility of industrial action by teachers concerning financial matters.

"Are youse gaun oan strike surr?" they had inquired of me when the first 'whiffs of grapeshot' had been fired by Pringle and Major regarding corridor duty.

I told Pringle that I had informed them in no uncertain manner of my views on striking and had made it abundantly clear that, contrary to countenancing such irresponsible action, I would do all in my power to ensure that senior staff were given every assistance in their efforts to maintain the continuation of all school activities.

"Perhaps," I queried Pringle, "they took umbrage at my remarks and decided to ostracize me with this anonymous graffiti — it's the kind of half-witted protest these under-achievers would make, isn't it?"

The poor old fellow seemed to be overtaken by a severe fit of coughing just as I'd finished speaking. He turned an alarming shade of red and had to bury his face in a rather tatty looking handkerchief for so long that I felt compelled to inquire of him whether he required the attentions of the school nurse.

Eventually he pulled himself together, assumed a solemn expression, and assured me of his wholehearted co-operation in my endeavours to locate the culprits. I thanked him profusely and went on my way.

It's good to know that inter-union differences on procedural matters don't cloud the essential humanity and professionalism of my colleagues.

pm

Took five minutes off my preparation period before the afternoon interval to grab a quick cup of coffee. No one has volunteered to assist with the corridor duty as yet but I'm managing to cope — so far!

As I approached the staffroom door I caught the hearty guffaws of several staff members and looked forward to sharing in the hilarity. Mr Pringle seemed to be in the middle of a particularly amusing story which was holding the attention of the assembled company but — as I entered — he broke off and was overtaken by an even more distressing respiratory attack; strange to relate, he could not be persuaded to continue with his anecdote — it's not very often that *he's* lost for words, I must say! Maybe Dickson, who was also present, could be persuaded to tell me what's going on.

Thursday 29th November

Not much today. I *had* been looking forward to attending an in-service course this evening on "Cloze Procedure Remediation For Socially Disadvantaged Pupils" but — owing to further bloody-mindedness over industrial action (again!) — the entire venture was called off. I was the only one to turn up and the adviser decided it wasn't worthwhile going ahead.

It's all very annoying.

Friday 30th November

A large crowd was gathered in the staffroom this morning when I arrived. The centre of attention appeared to be Dickson, the mod langs fellow who's been trying to get a job as a double-glazing salesman. Apparently he's been successful in what *I* would consider an extremely foolhardy venture and the rest of the staff were intent upon congratulating him on his "release".

It's quite ridiculous, really: several of the staff have formed what they are pleased to call an "Escape Committee" and spend the vast majority of their time making rather puerile jokes about "digging tunnels" and "getting out safe on the other side", as if they were in Colditz, for heaven's sake!

They were even going to hold an election for the new chairmanship of the escape committee, now that Dickson's due to go: apparently Mr Pickup of Geography is favourite for this exalted position.

I waited until all the hullabaloo surrounding Dickson had died down and sought him out alone this afternoon. Having offered my congratulations I nonetheless felt constrained to indicate my disapproval of his decision to leave.

"After all," I said, "there aren't many jobs where you get such security *and* job satisfaction into the bargain — not to mention the long holidays."

He threw me the most withering glance it has been my misfortune to receive in many a long year and said nothing. Realizing I had ventured into yet another "sensitive area" I hastened to ask him if, in the time left to him prior to his departure for "fresh fields and pastures new", he would see fit to lend some assistance in the search for my blackboard graffiti artists.

The fellow suddenly adopted the most ridiculous "cloak-and-dagger" appearance and, beneath his outstretched arm, hoarsely whispered: "Beware the foe within". . . .

I think it's as well he's leaving.

November — December 1984

Many young teachers used to think as Morris did. Weaned on a literary diet of Buckeridge and Delderfield, Morris still viewed teaching as a noble career, one in which the thinking adult could respond to the shifting challenges of adolescent wonder by channelling evanescent thoughts and energies towards the constant inculcation of respectable moral standards and the ceaseless quest for knowledge. Indeed, one of his favourite poetic quotations was Tennyson's exhortation "to strive, to seek, to find, and not to yield", and he seldom tired of repeating it to any of his classes prepared to remain silent long enough for him to impress upon them the wisdom of the poet's remarks.

In strong contrast, but with the same poem in mind, Alan Dickson was intent to "seek a newer world". Too young by far to join the ever lengthening queue of early-retirement-seekers who had given up their unequal struggles against pupil indiscipline and the educational sillinesses emanating from their superiors, Alan had decided to opt out at the early age of thirty one years. It was an escape viewed with a mixture of surprise and, as we have already seen, some envy by his colleagues at Parkland High: teaching had always been a vocation for Alan Dickson too, but he had come to the conclusion that, in Government eyes, the vocational animal was one with a very soft underbelly and little stomach for a fight. He'd watched it happen to the nurses and he was watching it happen to the teachers, drawn into a frantic vortex of diminishing salaries, stubbornly reluctant to utilise the one armoury weapon which would draw attention to their plight — strike action. As events were to demonstrate, the underbellies of teachers proved harder that most had predicted, but Alan wanted none of it.

His great joy in teaching, for joy it had once been, was the trust and rapport between himself and the pupils, the excitement of joining together in a genuine search for some kind of educational fulfillment, but his relaxed and dedicated approach to what was so much *more* than just a job had become increasingly strained of late. The demands for new courses, devised at his own expense and in his own time; the demise of effective disciplinary procedures for the very rare pupil who overstepped the mark in his classroom; the unceasing deluge of paperwork; the bitterness emerging from within at the constant requirement to give of himself entirely, utterly, with no offer of return; the sheer impossibility of supporting two children on a salary which would have been sufficient as a supplementary income only — for all of these reasons, then, Alan Dickson had regretfully decided to hang up his blackboard duster for good.

The decision once made, however, and his resignation once posted, Alan knew no regrets. His shoulders appeared unburdened and a lightness filled his step during those last few weeks of term. His mood was in sharp, sharp relief to the disenchantment evident among the remainder of staff, for whom a dismal Christmas approached, its financial demands clutching fiercely at their ever thinning wallets.

By the end of November the management side of the *SJNC* had produced a report on the teachers' workload which it intended to use as a lever in persuading the Government to abandon intransigence and prevarication. As a prelude to the national strike of December 5th, it could not have been more appropriate. Its conclusions that teachers were "under greater stress than they have ever been before" was greeted with sage acknowledgement in staffrooms across the country.

But still no announcement.

In a long planned demonstration of frustration at the endless procrastination of government, then, the *EIS* called their national strike for Wednesday 5th December. It was, by any account, the most widely supported strike action in Scottish educational history, adhered to by over 80% of the membership, crippling practically every secondary school in the country and closing vast numbers of primaries.

The gloves having been officially removed, George Younger therefore found himself able, on December 14th, to phrase his response to the request which had first been framed some 24 weeks previous.

To hardly anyone's surprise at all, the answer was a firm and definitive 'no'. The fact that he seemed intent to inflame matters further by suggesting they could "handle this another way", by mooting a deal based on a review of service conditions before offering *any* kind of financial settlement was regarded, by John Pollock, as "a dredged up version of Sir Keith's discredited proposals"*. Alex Stanley, of the *SSTA*, saw Mr Younger's response as "grossly inflammatory" and it wasn't difficult to see his reasoning. If Mr Younger was sincere in his remarks that an independent pay review would commit him to honouring a large blank cheque, was he not admitting that the review's recommendation would be for substantial salary increases? Was he not, in fact, admitting to the complete validity of the teachers' request?

No matter. The answer was no, and the troops entrenched for a long and bitter struggle. The *EIS* 'levy fund' stood at £500,000, and headquarter strategists laid plans to "target" certain areas of the country with unremitting strike action in the New Year. Schools within the constituencies of Conservative M.P.'s, especially those of Government Ministers, were to be hit by three-day strikes throughout the coming months, and *all* co-operation in non-contractual duties was to be withdrawn with immediate effect.

The concluding days of 1984 saw the provision of two in-service days, the final hangover from Standard Grade preparation. Parkland High School still found itself recovering from the industrial activities of the preceding two weeks, and Morris Simpson found himself thrust into a bewildering cauldron of rising tempers and vicious recrimination. Still infused with a desire to promote the cause of education, he seemed oblivious to the storm cones being hoisted in the distance, and concentrated his thoughts on reviewing his progress as a first-year probationer, for whom industrial action was a complete and utter irrelevance.

He found little sympathy.

Monday 17th December

Eighteen weeks into my teaching career I look back on a term of fascinating discovery and forward to a New Year full of educational challenge.

*Sir Keith Joseph, Secretary of State for Education in England and Wales, had proposed a similar deal for English teachers, whose campaign and demands were entirely different from those of their Scottish counterparts.

Today, however, the school was still recovering from the effects of the last two weeks' industrial action by members of Mr Pringle's union, action which closed the school for two entire days; additionally, in my opinion, it effectively jeopardised our pupils' future education. In fact, I said as much to the head last week and he readily concurred — hope he remembers my comments when he's writing my interim report on Friday!

Actually, as a member of a non-striking union, I also felt constrained to tell Pringle exactly what I thought of his group's somewhat militant stance, and took the opportunity as he staggered into the staffroom this morning with a large banner under each arm, the remnants of last week's demonstration.

"Morning, Mr Pringle," I called, but I don't think he heard because he walked straight past me. Scurrying in his direction, I tapped him on the shoulder whereupon he ground to a halt, swivelled his neck and fixed me with what I can only describe as an impatient frown.

"Yes. What is it?" he snapped.

Having explained I merely wanted a quick word, I 'laid the groundwork' by enquiring after the success of his demonstration.

"Fine," he said. "It went just fine. But it would have been a damned sight finer if you and some of the pussyfoots in Major's union had got off your backsides to come and join us!"

I was, I admit, stung by his aggressive attitude and launched into a scathing counter-attack wherein I indicated, quite forcibly, that in my opinion a responsible and professional body such as ours should *never* become involved in what are simply undignified public manifestations of discontent.

"Look, son," he confided, "you've been in this game for four months now and you've learned nothing." I opened my mouth to protest, but he held up his hand and continued: "If they want to call us a profession then it's about bloody time they started *paying* us like one!"

With that, he turned on his heel and lurched out of the room, a forlorn banner hanging limply from his arm

I sometimes wonder if Pringle really *enjoys* his job like I do.

Tuesday 18th December

Both Pringle and Major are still trying to get me to join their respective unions. I must say that Mr Major's arguments this morning *did* sound quite attractive. He pointed out, quite correctly, that I am "out on a limb" owing to the fact that I am the only member of my union in this school. Furthermore, he reminded me that his union, though smaller than Pringle's, was a sight cheaper to *join* and it was better equipped to look after my interests as a *secondary* school teacher. Most importantly for me, he said that as far as striking was concerned I needn't worry *too* much about that likelihood if I were to join his group.

Wednesday 19th December

A distressing occurrence on this, the last teaching day of term. Having decided to relax the normal routine with most of my classes, I had instructed them to bring in books of their own choice from home, the only stipulation being that their reading material should not consist of comics or annuals.

Imagine my horror, then, when carrying out a survey with the third year at Period 2, to discover one boy avidly perusing an extremely dog-eared copy of a book called, believe it or not, *Emmanuelle's Eastern Promise*. He protested that the said tome was a Biblical epic and, for a moment, I was taken in.

Closer investigation, however, revealed it to be nothing less than a thinly veiled text of pornographic excess. I told him I'd be sending a letter home, but he took me slightly by surprise by informing me that he'd filched it from his father's bookcase!

I have decided to let the matter rest.

Thursday 20th December

Today was the first "in-service" day of two which have been granted to us by the regional authority in order that we can get ahead with developmental work for some of the new courses.

I spoke to Major about it, hoping to locate a voice of sanity, but even *he* said that he certainly wasn't going to be dictated to by some "petty minded bureaucrat in a regional office who hasn't seen the inside of a classroom for 20 years"!

I disagreed and told him that *I* thought it was an extremely generous gesture on the part of the education authority. He seemed to lose his equilibrium for a moment and shouted, "Oh, don't be such a wimp, Simpson — the only gesture they've made to us in the last decade is one with two raised fingers and a very loud raspberry!"

I'm afraid I took umbrage at his somewhat inelegant remarks and told him that if this was an example of his union's brotherly solidarity then he certainly wouldn't be getting *my* subscription for the forthcoming year.

Friday 21st December

A disastrous conclusion to the first term of my teaching career! A large group of the staff had organized a celebratory lunch in a nearby hostelry and asked me to join them. Being naturally averse to such occasions, I declined, protesting that I had brought my cheese sandwiches as normal. Nothing loth, however, they insisted that I came along; after all, it was the last day of term as well as a chance to say farewell to Dickson, the fellow who's leaving teaching to become a double-glazing salesman. I relented, lest I hurt Dickson's feelings, and joined the party in what proved to be a somewhat disreputable public house.

I'm afraid I don't remember much of what happened next, though I clearly recall telling both Pringle *and* Dickson, in no uncertain terms, that I *never* drank more than one dry Martini at lunch-time, and I do remember thinking that my subsequent tomato juices tasted distinctly unusual. My next recollection, however, is that of waking up in the staffroom to discover myself stretched out along the sofa next to the tea-urn.

Glancing at my watch, I was horrified to learn that it was nearly 4 o'clock and turning my eyes towards the door I perceived the head and Pringle deep in earnest conversation.

"Well you've got to understand", Pringle was saying, "it's been quite a trying term for him. The poor lad's worked himself to the bone — he's just very, very . . . er . . . tired."

"Yes," mused the head between tightly pursed lips, casting a ferocious glance in the direction of my recumbent figure. "About as tired as a newt!"

With this valedictory remark he strode out of the staffroom and marched towards his study, no doubt selecting a few choice remarks for my end-of-term report.

Perhaps I can make a fresh start in the New Year. . . .

December 1984 —
January 1985

The month of January was, indeed, to prove something of a watershed in terms of Morris's future career. Still desirous to make a name for himself in education, he nevertheless gave much thought to his financial position over the Christmas break, and found himself unable to contemplate abandoning the parental nest — as had been his intention — for the independent responsibility of home-ownership. Mortgage repayments for a one-bedroomed flat would have been far beyond his means once other living expenses had been incurred, and the realisation that his weekly take-home pay amounted to a sum slightly below that given to him during his student holidays as a hospital porter came as something of a monetary shock.

Subsequent to the holiday period, his attention was also drawn to the widespread disaffection of many more teachers than he had hitherto imagined by the suddenly enlarged media attention being devoted to educational unrest. Despite having been in dispute for the past six and a half months, Scottish industrial action in schools was given scant notice by the national news bulletins until January '85. Even then, the difficulties north of the border were merely tagged on to the end of reports concerning the recently inflamed English teachers and their demands for a minimum increase of £1200 per annum to bring them within shouting distance of 1975 pay levels. The satisfaction of having at least had their existence acknowledged by supposedly national news networks was tinged with a good deal of frustration at the apparent provinciality of journalistic sympathies — but at least southerners now *knew* there was something going on in Scotland.

Sadly, there were few who could appreciate that Scottish demands were related to far more than a simple — if justifiable — bitterness at teachers' low salaries. A whole range of extra-contractual duties had long been taken for granted of teachers, and, although the job can actually be *enhanced* by involvement with school societies, sports clubs, youth groups and the like, it is surely unfair to expect them to be undertaken as an automatic duty; more contentious than running a school club, however, was the issue of a teacher based overhaul of the Scottish examination system.

Standard Grades, the replacement for 'O' Grades, had suffered an abnormally long gestation period already. First mooted in the Munn and Dunning Reports of the 1970s, these examinations aimed to give *every* school pupil the chance to achieve *some* form of certification by the time compulsory schooling was completed at the age of sixteen. Laudable aims, which met with general support, but whose implementation was to become a woeful catalogue of economic pussilanimity. Development of new courses, new forms of assessment, new methodologies, were all to come from the teachers themselves, and that was only correct: their expertise and knowledge of the teaching practicalities should have led to courses far more appropriate to pupil needs than courses bestowed from on high by a remote educational hierarchy.

Unfortunately, the missing factor in this equation was "teacher-time": materials had to be written at home; unpaid and time-consuming in-service courses had to be attended; entire schemes of work had to be revised and rewritten and, ultimately, working parties had to meet, consult, and recommend upon the adoption of 'grade related criteria', a central item of faith in the educational nirvana about to be offered to all schoolchildren. Instead of comparing pupils to each other on a scale of merit ('norm-referencing'), which tended to highlight what they could *not* do, assessments were to be conducted employing the more egalitarian principles of 'criterion-referencing', using a scale of seven main criteria designed to pinpoint what each child *could* do. Hence, a Grade 1 (Credit) candidate in English (Reading) could demonstrate in writing that he had a "firm grasp and sensitive appreciation of what he reads", whereas a Grade 3 (General) pupil would have merely "an adequate grasp of what he reads", while a Grade 6 (Foundation) child would possess only a "rudimentary grasp and appreciation of what he reads".

The complexities of Grade Related Criteria (GRC) became legion, and Mr Tod's frequently splenetic outlook could, in fact, often be attributed to the most recent demands he had received in connection with devising such criteria for the newly introduced "Social and Vocational Skills" course. How in God's name, he could be heard muttering, was he supposed to devise seven different grades to assess pupils on sticking wallpaper to a wall, or on making a pot of tea? The top and bottom grades in any subject were always relatively straightforward to formalise, but the subtle shades of accomplishment pertaining to the intervening categories proved frequently awkward to establish.

Whatever the merits and demerits of these matters, it was upon the long suffering class teacher that the burden of innovation and preparation was to fall, and it was the unremitting demands for educational reform to be bulldozed through under the most economic terms available — that is, as an 'extra' during the teachers' own time — which finally brought their frustration to the boil.

An (English) survey conducted by the *National Union of Teachers* in the four weeks prior to Christmas '84 had revealed that their members worked an average of 20.03 hours above their statutory 27 hours; in the months prior to their contractual work-to-rule, a substantial proportion of Scottish teachers felt that a working week of 47 hours would be an unaffordable luxury if pupil requirements were to be met properly!

The month of January, then, saw a hardening of attitudes in disputes on both sides of the border, particularly after the Government announced its plans to weed out incompetent teachers before offering *any* deals on pay. Teachers are the first to admit that there are bound to be incompetents among their number — just as there are in *any* profession — but militancy was no doubt increased by such ministerial pronouncements. Indeed, it was strongly felt that, had the Government conducted a similarly draconian exercise before awarding themselves *their* most recent pay increase, then the House of Commons would have found itself a much more solemn chamber.

The beginning of *SSTA* strikes in January, strikes by a union whose members were generally unwilling to flex industrial muscle, might have been an indication of the strength of feeling in academic quarters, but such sensitivity was never a hallmark of the Government concerned; what better example of this than yet another inflammatory statement from Allan Stewart who, commenting on *EIS* action, "deplored the perverse pleasure displayed by the *EIS* leadership in what it has done and proposes to do to damage educational developments in our primary and secondary schools, and its reiterated determination to use its power over pupils as a political weapon in its dispute with the government."

Such isolation from reality was stunning. There can be very few teachers who enjoy striking, and the implication that they were being used as pawns in some grander political and ideological struggle was little short of insulting. Perhaps, of course, it was just Mr Stewart's personal response to the *EIS* strategy, formalised on 10th January, of targeting schools within Government Ministers' constituencies, not least his own at Eastwood, Glasgow.

Meanwhile, the Scottish Education Department still hoped for the continuation of Standard Grade, and the most optimistic of educationists were still formulating plans for the post-Standard Grade era: working parties still met — if in something of a vacuum — to discuss proposed revisions to the Higher Grade examinations, in keeping with the philosophies of Standard Grade. The letter pages of the press resounded, briefly, with suggested titles for the new exams, titles which would indicate the superior academic achievements of successful candidates. Morris Simpson reckoned that this was a promotion bandwagon he could easily board, and submitted a *named* article to the *TESS*, outlining his thoughts on the subject. It was never printed.

By January, the Action Plan had also stuttered into sporadic life across Scottish schools, and certain teachers in Parkland remained confused by the sight of casually dressed college students appending themselves to classes of uniformed 16 year-olds.

But still uppermost in Morris's mind throughout the impecunious weeks of January '85 was the uninspiring salary cheque he would receive at the end of the month: at the weekly rate of approximately £84 after tax, it would not be quite enough to cancel his rapidly enlarging overdraft. He began to draw comparisons with what he understood to be the average police officer's pay packet — in the region of £160, also after tax, almost double his own. He began, also, to devote much attention to comparability studies which revealed that, in 1974, teachers' salaries had been on a par with those of computer programmers, accountants and electrical engineers; by 1984, these professions' salaries had risen by 300%, a figure which dwarfed the teachers' increases of 212%. Police pay had risen by 373% in the same period.

It was with such ruminations in mind that Morris entered the staffroom on the 21st of January. . . .

Monday 21st January

I have decided to make a stand over teachers' salaries and have joined Mr Major's union! I know this is contrary to my earlier intentions of remaining in a non-striking union but I feel it is time for something to be done.

What finally convinced me was a tale from Mr Pickup of Geography: this morning he informed the staffroom that he had received a visit from Cox, a boy in last year's fourth year who was, in his time, regarded as the educational equivalent of the Antichrist, and who left school with two O Grades, both in Home Economics!

Cox, it now transpires, is working as a hospital chef — and taking home £30 per week more than Pickup, who has been teaching for seven and a half years!

I knew teachers were badly paid but this revelation shocked me and I lost no time in approaching Mr Major with a completed membership form.

"Huh. You've changed your tune," he sneered, but I chose to ignore his cheap jibe and handed over my cheque for £11 probationary membership. At least his union is less likely to go on strike than Pringle's so I shouldn't lose *too* much pay if it comes to the bit!

Tuesday 22nd January

On strike.

Major omitted to inform me that my new union was to be on strike today despite being a "traditionally moderate" one. Having turned up at school this morning, then, I was redirected to the centre of town where a protest march was being held in support of our pay campaign.

It was really quite ridiculous: I had to barge through a phalanx of angry mothers protesting at *our* protest and eventually emerged to join the march having lost an arm from one side of my spectacles and peering through the broken lens in the other.

The march itself seemed to go off well enough. I think we provided an impressive show. A crocodile of very angry teachers waving banners and demanding action from the Government. Sadly, the impetus of the event was somewhat lessened when we had to stop at the Pelican crossing to get over the main road and our half-mile cavalcade was broken into several rather smaller units.

Still, it should have given the education authorities something to think about!

Wednesday 23rd January

Had to put up with some cheeky comments from the third year over my broken spectacles but I think I put them in their place. Not that there were many pupils, mark you: the vast majority of them appear to believe that, as my union was on strike yesterday and Pringle's is on strike tomorrow, they are perfectly entitled to consider the intervening 24 hours as an *extra* holiday.

If this is the attitude they display with regard to their schooling then I don't hold out very many hopes for their future careers.

Spent most of this evening preparing an article I intend submitting to the *TESS*. It's called "Post-Standard — The Imperial Grade?"

Thursday 24th January

A visit from Dickson, the fellow who left teaching to become a double-glazing salesman. He seems different, somehow. Apart from the very obvious acquisition of a new suit, his conversation seems singularly one-sided: all he could discuss was his forthcoming sales target and the "bonuses" he was due to receive should he achieve it.

Sadly, he appears to have lost all interest in education.

Friday 25th January

Despite having been in the school for nearly five full months, I still experience occasional difficulty over the geography of the place.

Today was a case in point. Lost in a maze of thought

concerning my bottom fourth year and the possibility of practising on them with some of the behaviour modification theories I learned in college, it was with no small measure of surprise that I found myself outside a strange door labelled: "The upper staffroom — abandon all hope ye who enter here."

Raucous laughter emerged as I peered around the door and gazed upon what seemed a frightful den of iniquity: three men and two women, all dressed in track suits and training shoes, were lounging across four armchairs, enjoying the remnants of a bottle of red wine and apparently relishing the delights of some strongly flavoured cigarettes.

"Sorry. Wrong room," I muttered, and scurried away in an effort to hide my confusion.

I spoke about it to Mr Pringle later on, and asked him whether the room had been given over to students from the local further education college who were here "on a module".

"Good God, no, Simpson," he snorted. "That's the beanbaggers' staffroom."

"Beanbaggers?" I inquired.

"Yes. The PE staff. That's where they hide away. They were probably holding a departmental meeting when you burst in. That's the only time when two or three of *them* are ever gathered together. They're a bit upset at the moment 'cos the head's insisting on having a proper course for first and second year so they can justify their marks on the report card at the end of term. Instead of letting the kids run round the gym all day till they fall down sick they're having to work out seven grade related criteria for jumping over a wall or something. It's the first piece of work any of them have had to do since they came here."

"They didn't look very interested in it when *I* walked in! And their clothes! Does the head actually *allow* them to dress so casually?"

"No choice, my boy," Pringle confided. "He tried to kick up a stooshie about it last year but they threatened to stop running all the football and hockey teams, so he wasn't having *that*. A lot of prestige in football trophies, y'know."

Education seems to have changed since my day. . . .

46

February — March 1985

Education had indeed changed since Morris's day, recent though that day undoubtedly was, and perhaps the change was nowhere more marked than in the eternally controversial issue of corporal punishment.

Since August 1983 the use of a 'tawse', or 'belt', had been specifically banned as an instrument of discipline in most Scottish schools. The catalyst for this eventual action within Strathclyde had been the case raised in the European Court of Human Rights by a Clydebank mother: Mrs Grace Campbell refused to allow corporal punishment to be inflicted on her son, took the case to Strasbourg, won it — thus tolling the death knell for the belt in Strathclyde — and then removed her son to a private school, where corporal punishment was still enforced!

For the beleaguered teacher, it was another source of irritation. There were probably more wrongs than rights to corporal punishment, but it *had* provided an ultimate weapon in the battle to maintain classroom order. Used injudiciously, it was perhaps a barbaric form of keeping discipline, and it wasn't really its abolition which distressed teachers so much as the unilateral injunction to cease its use forthwith and the complete absence of any alternative sanction with which to punish persistent troublemakers. Staff were left to fall back on punishment exercises and exclusion orders.

With regard to the former, the issuing, recording and collection of such exercises proved to be an administrative nightmare for any uncertain teacher, and the curt refusal of a recalcitrant pupil to produce the said punishment could only be countered with the lame threat to hand out another punishment — and another, and another, and another! The latter sanction, suspension from school, was effectively the only alternative: schools were to be granted the authority to exclude pupils, and suspensions could range between one and three days for relatively minor — but repeated — misconduct, while misdemeanours of a more serious nature could lead to suspensions of several weeks, or even months. Correctly enough, written evidence of previous and repeated misbehaviour had always to be provided if pupils were to be deprived of their education, but the voluminous tracts of triplicate paperwork often necessary to set these events in motion were daunting enough to allow flagrant breaches of conduct to go frequently unchecked.

In any case, the one serious flaw in this system would appear to have been the fact that, strange as it may seem, suspension from school was not regarded as a punishment by those pupils most likely to suffer from it. Morris's Geographical colleague, Mr Pickup, was heard on more than one occasion berating an educational system which chose to punish those pupils with an intense dislike of school by offering them the chance to misbehave so atrociously that they could be rewarded with a legal obligation to cease attendance! " Bugger suspension!" he would repeat time and time again: "Hit their parents where it hurts — in the pocket! Do like the Froggies, and chop off their family allowance if Junior steps out of line. Either that," he would continue menacingly, "or introduce a programme of mass sterilisation for the lower orders so they can't keep churning out assembly lines of the vicious little bastards we seem to get lumbered with here!"

Tolerance was not one of Mr Pickup's virtues.

Another area of wholesale change in the school curriculum since Morris's "day" was the mass introduction of computer education into schools throughout the early 1980's. Education Authorities, stung by Industry's plaintive barbs about the irrelevance of education to society's needs, suddenly located hitherto untapped sources of wealth to purchase vast batallions of computers and all their associated paraphernalia of printers, software and network systems.

An interesting proportion of teachers were momentarily disadvantaged by their computer-literate pupils, whose parents had all provided them with such machines several years previous, but secretive sessions alone at the monitor soon provided the chance to catch up. A new vocabulary emerged in staffrooms as the benefits of the 'Apple' computer were weighed against those of the 'Apricot', and as Mr Pickup mooted the possibility of setting up a Senior Girls' Computing Class in Parkland High, the term "hands-on experience" began to acquire whole new shades of meaning, not entirely unconnected with his widely recognised admiration for Amanda Torrance of the 5th Year. . . .

But of course the disaffection continued, as *EIS* targeting increased in both ferocity and frequency, and a joint *EIS/SSTA* petition with 150,000 signatures attached was presented at Downing Street. The *NAS/UWT* (National Association of Schoolteachers/Union Of Women Teachers) launched strike action in Strathclyde during February as well as lodging an interim pay demand for a 17.5% increase, whilst Morris's ex-union, the *PAT*, felt that "unions should start to negotiate on what has so far been offered by the Government and local education authorities." This initiative met with little support.

The vast majority of Scottish teachers were more firmly convinced than ever that an independent pay review was the only just and effective means of resolving their dispute and setting Scottish education on an even, secure keel for the future. The Prime Minister, however, was not so well informed: questioned in the Commons by Tom Clark, Monklands West Labour M.P., she rejected such a review for Scottish teachers — with a commendably detailed grasp of the *English* teachers' dispute.

"The teachers' pay claim," she answered him peremptorily, "is a minimum flat rate increase of £1200 per teacher which would cost about six hundred million pounds. The employers have offered arbitration and they have refused. I see no reason for an independent enquiry."

The employers had offered Scottish teachers no such thing, for no such claim had been made by them, but Mrs Thatcher's response provided illumination on the Government's knowledge of — and commitment to solving — the eight month old dispute in Scotland.

Those teachers who could — like Alan Dickson — left for other jobs. If new employment prospects were unlikely or unattractive, there was always the ever-ripening carrot of early retirement.

Another, previous, Commons question of December '84 had revealed that 745 teachers had been granted early retirement by Scottish education authorities in the five months between April and August of that year; comparative figures for previous years were "not readily available", but the underlying sentiment within all schools was that the figure was undoubtedly higher than before, and that the growth in such requests would soon reach epidemic proportions.

Mr Douglas, Headmaster of Parkland High, was a Touchstone who longed for an honourable retreat at the somewhat premature age of 57. Twenty-six years of teaching had not prepared him for the wholesale changes being wrought in his school at the behest of local authorities and regional councillors, and much of his recent time had been spent in the preparation of lengthy documents which detailed his case for early retirement to the staffing department and his Divisional Education Officer.

By March of '85, a positive response had at long last been issued, and Mr Douglas had little patience to consider the disciplinary problems of a first-year probationer. Morris, unaware of his headmaster's intentions to depart the profession, felt slightly bewildered as he went seeking professional advice.

Monday 24th March

An appointment with the headmaster over a disciplinary matter which has given me cause for concern. He seemed in an unusually jovial mood for a Monday morning and did not appear inclined to give my problem much serious consideration.

"It's like this, headmaster," I told him, "I've had just about enough of young Maxwell's cheek. Why, only last Friday I caught him smoking behind the lunch-hall. Not only did the little hooligan refuse to extinguish the cigarette, but he had the temerity to offer one to *me!*"

"Give the little sod a punishment exercise," was his only constructive suggestion.

"But that's the trouble. I've already *given* him three in the last two weeks and he's yet to hand in *any* of them."

"Well . . . give him another."

"But headmaster — "

"Sorry, Simpson," he interrupted. "Can't waste any more time on this one. Got to get upstairs — just about to take delivery of our new computer."

Distracted for a moment, I confessed my ignorance of the new arrival.

"Oh, yes," he chortled, "Newest model on the market — the Prune 463 . . . " and with this parting shot he scurried away down the corridor pressing a handkerchief against his face.

Mentioned the computer to Mr Major this afternoon: he

informed me that no such machine was available: "Strange to say, the old boy must have been having a joke," he confided. "I must say, he *has* been looking very cheerful today — he normally sees jokes by appointment only."

The mystery deepens.

Tuesday 25th March

All is revealed.

Apparently the headmaster has been granted early retirement at the third time of asking and is due to leave at the end of this session. It seems rather a shame that a man of his undoubted commitment and enthusiasm should want to leave the educational system at a time of such exciting development and innovation, and even sadder that he seems so gleeful about the whole business.

Wednesday 26th March

The head's world has collapsed around his ears! Having spent the last two days in a mood of positively unwholesome exuberance, he was observed storming from the school office to his study at ten minutes past nine this morning. Half an hour of telephoning later he emerged with an expression of ferocious animosity upon his brow. Apparently the school is to be visited by Her Majesty's Inspectorate within the next six weeks!

Interestingly enough, the news of the inspection has obviously been of value from my point of view: by half past ten I had been informed that Maxwell's father has been called in and that we are to have a frank exchange of views tomorrow.

Thursday 27th March

A positively disastrous session with Mr Maxwell and the head this afternoon. The boy's father, a burly man smelling strongly of drink, viewed me with intense suspicion from the beginning of the interview, and I don't think the head aided matters when he introduced me as "the new teacher your son seems to hate so much". Believe it or not, things got even worse.

I began by telling Mr Maxwell that his son seemed to have difficulty in relating to authority and that he seemed overassertive in a peer group situation. The man appeared unable to refute my allegations so I pressed home the advantage.

"What's more, Mr Maxwell," I continued, "Robert is a classic example of the under-achiever: his limited reasoning ability is further hampered by an extremely short concentration span. I frequently have to issue stern verbal reprimands but, when these appear to have little or no effect, I have little choice other than to issue a punishment exercise, which seldom . . . "

"Haud on! Haud on!" interjected Mr M. "Whit the hell are ye talkin' aboot? Verbal *whit?* Listen, son — if the boay's no daein' his lessons, jist belt im wan acroass the lugs. That's whit ah always dae."

"Mr Maxwell!" I protested. "Physical reprimands of that nature are expressly forbidden by the General Teaching Council. Indeed," I continued, "the use of corporal punishment has long been outlawed by the profession and . . . "

"Oh speak English for God's sake, Simpson," the head cut in. "Mr Maxwell hasn't come here to listen to a monologue from teacher training college. Just tell him what you want his son to do —"

I was astonished at this outburst but, before I could open my mouth in defence, Mr Maxwell had risen from his chair and forced his way through the study door, muttering comments the while about a "bunch of bloody comedians in Batman suits".

If that was an example of parental liaison then it's little wonder that education is in such a sorry state — and even less wonder that Maxwell has such an appalling academic record!

Friday 28th March

Had to call in at the cash dispenser on my way to school to collect some extra money for a strike levy we have been asked to pay by the union; consequently I was a little late in my arrival this morning but had the good fortune to apprehend two boys from my form class who were obviously intent on playing truant for the day: both were fully kitted out with fishing equipment as they waited for a No 16 bus!

"Right boys," I called out. "Over here!"

Smirking from ear to ear they sauntered over, so I spoke firmly and decisively.

"Into school. With me. Now!"

"But sir!" they protested.

"No buts. Bring those rods and we'll see what Mr Tod has to say about *this!*"

Muttering veiled threats about detention upon our arrival at the school gates, I quickly frogmarched the pair to the depute head.

"Caught these two about to have an early weekend, Mr Tod," I declared, looking forward to the congratulatory remarks which I felt certain were bound to follow.

Instead, the depute pulled me sharply aside and hissed "Don't be so wet Simpson. These two were *suspended* last week. They're not *allowed* to come into school". Turning from my crestfallen face, he curtly dismissed the boys, warning them not to come near the school for another two weeks.

"T . . . Terribly sorry Mr Tod," I stuttered in my confusion. "I . . . I . . . didn't know they'd been suspended. Must have missed it in the bulletin."

"Yes, Simpson," he replied acidly, "You miss rather a lot of things in the bulletin. Perhaps you ought to try and keep a little more up to date."

"Certainly, Mr Tod," I concurred. "Sorry about it all."

"Um . . . incidentally," I continued as he began to walk away, "— what were those two suspended *for?*"

"Playing truant, of course. Don't you ever find out about *anything?*"

Speechless, I watched Mr Tod march sternly to his next class. Perhaps I misheard him.

April — May 1985

Morris had *not* misheard Mr Tod, of course, for the sanction of suspension was indeed the ultimate punishment for the crime of truancy, a strange anomaly which had escaped the attention of the otherwise astute young probationer. The strain of his job was perhaps beginning to tell upon him, a likelihood indicated by his willingness to withdraw money for a levy which his own union had not even asked him to pay!

The *SSTA* found it unnecessary to extract cash from their membership in order to finance the less intensive action to be undertaken by this traditionally moderate union; in contrast, the *EIS* had organised a monthly levy from members, levels of contribution being dependent upon salary, in order to allow sustained and paid action in targeted and other chosen areas of Scotland. Their campaign looked set for a lengthy duration, and the wisdom of ensuring its adequate financing soon became apparent.

After the Easter holiday of April '85, the *EIS* announced a change of focus in its campaign. In an apparent fit of benevolence, a respite was to be granted to targeted secondary schools and attention was to be directed towards the Primary Sector prior to the SCE examination period. Commentators willing to accord altruistic motives to this decision commended the leadership for their commitment to ensuring that pupil examinations could proceed unhindered; more cynical reporters were heard to remark that — as all senior pupils are traditionally excused classes during this block of exams — it would have been foolish of teachers to pass up the annual opportunity to recharge batteries and tidy up classroom store cupboards during the extra free periods which would now come their way. It was an opportunity which Mr Major always anticipated with relish.

Whatever the reasons behind the change of emphasis in the campaign, however, the effects — and the very notion — of targeted action were still seen as an obvious source of irritation to Government officials, even after the respite was announced. Allan Stewart, never one to leave a fire smouldering when the opportunity existed to fan it back into life, branded the *EIS* targeting as a "quite unprecedented tactic of victimisation" and "a unique and disgraceful policy".

For once, John Pollock found himself in almost total agreement with the Scottish Minister for Education: indeed, he admitted that it was 'unfair and discriminatory' — but "no more so than the Government's policies on teachers' pay, on Scottish education, and on unemployment."

In any case, the success of the tactic could best be appraised by the incredible upsurge of interest in parents' meetings held in the halls of targeted schools: prior to targeting, such 'information evenings' would be lucky to draw upwards of twenty bodies; subsequent to targeting, it would be 'standing room only' as the dispute came to mean something personal and *real* to those citizens represented by Government Ministers in Parliament. Unfair the tactic may have been, but it *did* succeed in ensuring maximum attention for the teachers' case.

The Government, however, could perhaps afford to be embarrassed, for it spoke from a position of immense strength. At the beginning of March, Mrs Thatcher had at long last 'seen off' the miners, whose year-old pit strike had been smashed unceremoniously. Throughout the nation's staffrooms, mutterings were concealed behind the tea-urns: if the miners couldn't win, what hope had the teachers?

Even the Government's most recent attempt to shoot itself in the foot had ended in something akin to triumph for Mr Younger, yet the Scottish Rates Crisis of March and April had looked likely, at one time, to signal the final collapse of *all* Tory support north of the Border.

Scottish rates revaluation had been a thorny subject in the past, of course: it still seemed unfair to Scottish ratepayers that their rates could be 'revalued' at six to seven-yearly intervals, yet inhabitants of England and Wales had not experienced *any* such reappraisal during the past twelve years; it seemed unfair that the rates bills of some Scottish householders should suddenly be tripled — and even Sir James Goold, Chairman of the Conservative Party in Scotland, was subject to a rates demand which had increased from £959 to £1279 at the stroke of an assessor's biro; it seemed unfair that in Edinburgh, where some household rates bills were set to rise by 79%, one public-house owner received a rates demand which had risen from £1,427 to £9,226 in one fell swoop!

Eventually, of course, an astute awareness of the electoral consequences likely to be reaped persuaded Mr Younger to mount a search for an extra £38½ million, a search which concluded with the truly amazing discovery of an extra £50 *million* in rate support grants. The Tory strongholds were mollified, and Mr Younger's position of strength assured for the May Conference of the Scottish Conservatives in Perth.

Surprisingly enough, it seemed unlikely that such a pot of gold would be uncovered in time to provide a hasty end to the ten month old teachers' dispute: by March 25th, *The Glasgow Herald* reported, Mr Younger had told the Scottish Grand Committee that the teachers' industrial action was "utterly pointless" because there was no prospect of an independent pay review: "We have no intention," he outlined firmly, "of handing decisions on this important element in public expenditure over to a group of people with no familiarity with the subject and no responsibilities for finding the money to finance the deal they recommend . . . "

Not everyone saw it that way, of course. At the (English) National Union of Teachers' Conference in Scarborough during early April, Gordon Green, *NUT* President, paid "tribute to our friends in the *EIS* in Scotland who have mounted a brilliant and sustained campaign north of the border", and the Scottish Office announcement (during the second week of April) to the effect that schools could now decide for themselves on whether to present for the new exams or for 'O' Grades in 1986 left the Standard Grade edifice as an officially sanctioned ruin, a listed building propped up by the ironic willingness of the strike-free independent sector to maintain it as a going concern.

If teachers wished to recommit themselves to action, they needed only to scan the recently released pay data from the Burnham Committee in England, which highlighted the complete dearth of promotion opportunities in the profession as well as the fact that — had the Government held to its Election pledges to maintain teacher pay at 'Houghton levels', then a teacher at the top of the English Scale 1 *would* be earning £10,707 — not £8,556 — per annum.

In Scotland the *TESS* reported an interesting tale from Oban High School, whence another teacher had followed the path of Alan Dickson into double-glazing salesmanship: his previous annual salary of just over £6000, so the story went, began to pale into insignificance beside the £1200 commission he had recently made on one sale alone. The thoughts of John MacKay, formerly Principal Teacher of Mathematics at Oban, and staunch fighter in the pay campaigns of the 70's, but now a Scottish Office Minister, were not recorded on this occasion.

As a further demonstration of solidarity, the 24th of April saw another national strike which crippled Scottish Secondary schools, only five of which remained unaffected from a grand total of 434. 10,099 Strathclyde teachers out of 13,000 withdrew their labours for the day, and 116,750 Strathclyde pupils out of 181,000 were sent home.

Morris, although obliged to take part in the strike, nevertheless found himself increasingly embarrassed at becoming involved with such insensitive and unbecoming behaviour. His main concern, as the end of April approached, was to ensure that the pupils in his 4th Year Class — the only Certificate Group entrusted to him by Miss Bowman — were adequately prepared for their 'O' Grade in English. The lightening evenings saw him thrust deeper still into marking of pre-examination 'practice papers' which he had allocated for homework, though he found himself distressed at the barely literate standard of composition and essay writing which his pupils were proving able to achieve.

More distressing still, to the young probationer, was the discovery that he made in the duplicating room one Spring afternoon. . . .

It had been an idea he'd dreamed up during morning break, and Morris felt sure that a dramatic reconstruction of trench conditions in the 1st World War would help his young charges to sympathise with the experiences of Owen and Sassoon, thereby enabling them to analyse more closely and effectively the poetic achievements of both men in the literature section of their examination.

The "group stimulus" chart which he required to duplicate was a quickly devised document, but he was frustrated in his efforts to obtain 30 copies by the all-consuming activities of Mr Pringle at the Xerox machine: his departmental colleague, eyes fixed and apparently possessed, was intent upon recycling 30 copies each of two essays entitled, respectively, "War Writings — A Theme Study" and "A Poem I Have Read And Enjoyed".

Thirty sheets of A4 later, Morris — having discovered the

nature of Pringle's duplicated sheets — was moved to launch a bitter attack on the dishonesty of such 'exam-coaching', as he called it.

"Dishonesty?" countered Pringle. " Maybe so, but it sure as hell gets them through the paper, Simpson, and that's all that matters."

"Oh, Mr Pringle!" barked Morris: "Don't be so ridiculous. The literature part of their 'O' Grade urges all pupils to make a *genuine personal response* to the text they're discussing. It's blatantly criminal to —"

"Look, son," Pringle interrupted harshly, " — the only personal response these little toe-rags are capable of is in answer to a swift kick up the backside; as we're not allowed to do that anymore, I think it's as well they got some help in writing about the only poetry any of them're likely to read between here and their death-beds!"

Morris was amazed at Pringle's cynical approach to the teaching of literature; amazed at Pringle's suggestion that none of his pupils would ever read poems after they'd left school; amazed to think that Pringle actually *primed* his pupils for exams by preparing model essays which were then 'mugged up' and regurgitated during the examination itself; and amazed to learn that such an experienced teacher could actually countenance *cheating* at an examination. He clamped his jaws together and bided his time for the use of the photocopier. Pringle having extracted his final copy, he reached forward to insert his own 'master copy'.

"Sorry, old boy," Mr Pringle raised his arm. "Just got to do another 30 of each for Mr Major. Won't be a tick."

"But you don't mean!" exploded Morris, "that Mr Major uses these appalling . . . "

"Oh yes," murmured Mr Pringle, swiftly adjusting the toning device on the photocopier, "we've shared these kind of things for yonks now. Call it co-operative teaching if you like, twenty years before its time," he concluded, a contented smile of accomplishment spreading across his parted lips as he set the machine into noisy motion.

His expression set into firm lines of disapproval, Morris awaited his turn; before long, Pringle collected his batch of essays and, with a cheery wave, bade his young colleague farewell. Sadly, his duplicating enthusiasms had left the feeder

58

tray bereft of copying paper, and Morris was forced to request further supplies from Mrs Thomson in the school office. Her explanation that spending cuts had left *her* devoid of paper for the rest of the month brooked little sympathy with Morris, whose conviction that he was the innocent victim of some dire educational plot was assuming paranoiaic proportions.

In part, he was probably correct, but Mrs Thomson's revelation had been founded on truth. Indeed, spending cuts had dictated a whole host of financial short-cuts in recent years: it had been some eight months since Lothian Region had introduced an innovative cost-saving scheme relating to the removal of graffiti from the walls of educational establishments. The essence of the policy — which had aroused no small measure of media attention when first unfolded in August of '84 — was that graffiti should henceforth only be removed if judged to be obscene or likely to offend.

Councillor Keith Simpson, as recorded by *The Glasgow Herald*, complained that the injunction was "absolutely ridiculous", a charge difficult to deny, but countered valiantly by Alan Manning, then assistant divisional education officer for East Lothian, which division had "been operating a wind-and-water tight policy for repairs and maintenance". Consequently, he explained, it would now be "up to repair and maintenance staff" to decide if graffiti was to be removed, because it was obscene, or left.

Such thoughts of potential economies took a long time to filter through the rest of the Scottish Education System, but Parkland High School, like many others, was not immune from the attentions of anonymous graffiti artists and, as we shall learn, the dilemma had to be faced eventually.

Other dilemmas which confronted the Board Of Studies at Parkland were connected primarily with the impending visit of Her Majesty's Inspectorate. While many of the staff dreaded such an imposition, Morris found himself positively *looking forward* to the visitation. Here was a chance, he realised, to break out of the educational backwater to which he'd been posted, and impress the Inspectorate with some of the sterling project work he was embarking upon.

With The SCE Examination period looming, however, not everyone felt quite so enthusiastic.

Monday 5th May

With my senior pupils excused from classes during the present examination period I find myself with a substantially larger allocation of preparation time than hitherto. I look forward to catching up on a lot of first and second year assessment work as well as putting the finishing touches to a new humanities course I have devised for multi-ethnic third year pupils of mixed ability.

Mentioned my plans to Mr Major this afternoon, but he gave me what can only be described as an old-fashioned look and launched into a monologue of barely-suppressed scepticism.

"You *What?*" he laughed. "Come off it, Simpson. These three weeks comprise what can be loosely described as 'the perk of teaching': having given the best of our minds to our post-pubescent charges over the past nine months we can now send the little buggers over the top to face their exams alone — while we sit back at base, put our feet up, and organize a Scrabble championship! Don't tell me you're planning to *work* when they're away?"

I didn't want to appear *too* much of a damp squib, so I muttered a fairly non-committal response, while making a mental resolution to avoid his and his colleagues' appalling misuse of their free time. Scrabble championship indeed!

Tuesday 6th May

The visit of HMI, which commenced yesterday, has given Major and Pringle cause to move their lexical coterie to the upper staffroom, a God-forsaken hole removed from prying eyes. I have mentally reasserted my intention to remain aloof from their somewhat immature shenanigans, particularly after my unfortunate dealings with one of the aforementioned Inspectors this morning.

The man had turned up in my classroom looking for directions to the head's office and his arrival could not have been more ill-timed. Having just completed a scalding and scathing denunciation concerning the personal cleanliness and tidiness of the second year's most disreputable urchin, Lamont, I had been somewhat embarrassed to have this same boy draw attention to the open condition of my trouser flies. Class 2N, never the most disciplined of groups, seemed to derive great amusement from my misfortune and were in the process of giving vent to their hilarity when Mr Pratt selected his moment of entry.

He was, I suspect, taken aback by the uproarious chaos which greeted him and, endeavouring to hide my confusion, I hurriedly diverted him to the head's study. Apparently I misdirected him in my excitement, as Mr Pringle later informed me. It was he who had been on hand, I gather, in time to extricate the poor man from the brushes, mops and pails stored in the cleaner's cupboard whither I had sent him.

Wednesday 7th May

A feather in my cap today! Mr Tod, the depute head, has seen fit to give me sole responsibility for stage lighting at the school concert this year. He told me of his decision at morning break.

I did protest that my knowledge of electricity was strictly limited to the correct wiring of a 13 amp plug, but he said that this was more than the last fellow responsible for the job had known and that consequently I would be ideal.

I could hardly wait to tell my colleagues about this "mini-promotion" but none of them seemed to think it a very attractive proposition. Mr Pringle, in fact, likened the post to a "ruddy great albatross round the neck" and confided that Dickson, the fellow who left teaching at Christmas to become a double-glazing salesman, had been the last member of staff to "get landed with the job", as he put it.

Thursday 8th May

Mr Pringle's union had called a strike for today: although my own union was not out it meant there were very few staff and even fewer pupils in the school; indeed, the building seemed strangely at peace.

All seemed quiet, then, until the head ventured into the corridors during his morning patrol, a responsibility which he seems to have taken to heart since the beginning of industrial hostilities. This morning, unfortunately, he chanced upon the fourth year boys' cloakroom wall whereon a peculiarly apt caricature of himself had been inscribed.

Apparently, the muted growls of anger which emerged from a

61

a pair of very tightly pursed lips soon transformed themselves into a fearsome howl of near-bestial proportions when his eyes strayed to the legend, "The Heidie's A Poof", neatly lined in delicate filigree handwriting beneath the portraiture.

His wrath, understandably stirred by the initial sighting of what I must describe as a forlorn and childish attempt at humour, was compounded further upon the non-appearance of janitorial assistance to remove the offending graffiti. According to the Janitor, he is not allowed to remove graffiti from school property unless it is obscene and therefore likely to cause offence; he claimed, to the head's agitation, that this was in line with recent spending cuts and that, as the inscription could hardly be judged obscene, he would be constrained to leave it where it stood.

The head argued, with some justification, that in *his* eyes it was most *certainly* obscene but the Janitor remained unmoved. "Ah'm sorry, sir," he declaimed, "but it wid be mair than ma joab's worth tae try an' scrub that oaff. It's nae dirty enough, y'see."

Clutching a hand to his brow, the head retreated to his study, reminding me most particularly of a strong tree, straining against the wind and liable to snap at any moment.

Friday 9th May

The janitor's dilemma has been resolved: by 9.15 this morning he was to be observed forging a path towards the fourth year cloakroom, armed with a stiff brush and a bottle of cleaning solution. His position had been clarified, apparently, by the recent addition of several extremely florid adjectives to the mural's text as well as one or two emendations to the caricature's physical appearance which had altered, in the Janitor's eyes, the whole complexion of the matter.

Mr Pickup of Geography — who had discovered the updated version — reported that even he, an ex-Army man, had been surprised at the crudity of the appendages engrafted to the caricature; furthermore, he confessed, it had been a long time since he had witnessed linguistic extremities as bold and forthright as the string of Anglo-Saxon pronouncements employed to describe the headmaster in the latest piece.

We were discussing the matter over the Scrabble game this

afternoon and I *was* about to mention that, as the last teacher out of the building yesterday, I had met the head outside my classroom, a somewhat furtive expression on his face and a red felt pen clutched firmly between his palms. I decided, however, that discretion might be advisable on this occasion.

Loyalty is a virtue which I have always treasured. I trust it will be rewarded.

May — June 1985

Mr Douglas, however, had other things on his mind than rewarding loyalty which he would, in any case, have regarded as his due. The possibility that Her Majesty's Inspectorate might cloud his final months at the helm were a source of greater concern than the somewhat extravagant doubts cast upon his sexuality in the 4th Year cloakroom.

Certainly, the inspectors could be fully expected to take account of the unusual, strike-laden atmosphere and the consequent lack of curriculum initiative, but it still seemed unfair to Mr Douglas that the inspection had been arranged so close to his impending departure.

Alerted to possible areas of HMI criticism by rectorial colleagues in neighbouring schools, he had done his utmost to ensure that adequate supplies of toilet paper were available in all cloakrooms; nevertheless, he couldn't help wishing that the implementation of a core curriculum for 1st and 2nd Years — a wearisome task, so long delayed — could be effected so quickly and as painlessly as the bulk purchase of five cases of Andrex (for the staff) and thirty cases of Izal (for the pupils).

For the rest of the staff, however, HMI's departure meant nothing more than a chance to relax at last, and get on with the real work of furthering their pay campaign.

No longer in possession of the trump card which said "pay up or we'll screw the exams", the exams having been well and truly sat, teachers everywhere widely acknowledged the fact that they were digging in for a second year of dispute.

In the third week of May, lest morale was perceived to be flagging, Mr Pringle commandeered the Xerox machine once more and distributed seventy copies of a letter issued to local authorities in March.

The S.E.D., with all the tact and sensitivity for which it was fast becoming renowned, had suggested a number of measures to off-set teachers' strike action: education authorities had been asked, among other things, to consider rearranging timetables for 'O' and 'H' Grade pupils, to opening schools during the Easter holidays, recruiting temporary tutors and, where appropriate, giving financial assistance for pupils to receive private tuition.

Malcolm Green, the aforementioned Education Committee Chairman in Strathclyde, had gone on record in describing the documents as "unhelpful in the present circumstances" and, so far as can be discovered, few authorities took up the suggestions with relish.

Two months after its issue, the letter's greatest impact — in Parkland High School at any rate — was to confirm waverers in the faith of pursuing their action until it was won. And the possibility of some kind of ultimate victory was becoming more and more tangible as the strength of the *EIS* increased.

Since 1975, when the *EIS* membership had accounted for only 58% of Scottish teachers, mainly in the Primary sector, the roll had risen dramatically, until John Pollock could claim leadership, in 1985, of nearly 80% of all Scottish teachers.

A comparison between the position of the *EIS* and its closest counterpart in England, the National Union of Teachers, goes a long way towards explaining the respective strengths of each campaign: with just over 50% of English and Welsh teachers affiliated to the ranks of the *NUT*, it was a relatively easy matter, later in the year, for Sir Keith Joseph to reallocate seats on the Burnham Committee, nudge a few *NUT* members off the end of the bench, and make pay negotiations a relatively straightforward matter — from a Government point of view, at least. No such goalpost-shifting was possible north of the border, however, where one union held such a power base, so that the third week of May saw 1000 Primary Teachers and 20,000 of their pupils temporarily removed from the education system in twenty five small towns throughout the country.

Few teachers seemed to agree with Allan Stewart's assessment that the *EIS* leadership was asking members to "act like kamikaze pilots"; few put much faith in Mr Younger's sudden willingness to negotiate a pay and conditions package — a package attached to a very prominent label which said: "Little Money Available This Year"; few were impressed with David Semple's request, as Director of Education to his Lothian Headmasters, to provide a list of teachers who were refusing to submit order of merit forms to the Scottish Examination Board, a request which shouted "inquisition" to at least three Lothian

Heads who had subsequent pay slips docked for refusing to comply.

After ten months of dispute, then, the guerrilla warfare continued. Among the sporadic bursts of sniper fire, perhaps the following cross-exchange was symptomatic of the vast gulf existing between the two sides by the end of May 1985:

Ian Halliday, Depute Director of Strathclyde, had attempted to "put down a marker" with regard to the duties of employees during their long-sacrosanct 200 minutes of non-contact time; hitherto, he announced, it was the official view that this time would be "at the authority's disposal, not the teacher's".

In other words (it was felt in certain quarters), we are no longer prepared to treat you as adults: you *can* have 200 minutes when you're not actually teaching — but *we'll* tell you how you're going to use it. Bob Beattie, John Pollock's understudy at the *EIS*, aptly condensed the average teacher's response:

"There's nothing worse than people like Halliday — and me — pontificating about matters of this kind. The longer you're away from the classroom, the easier the job looks."

The two sides entrenched.

At their annual conference in Ayr, the *NAS/UWT* passed a motion to table a claim for restoration of salaries to at least *part* of their 'Houghton' levels. Arithmeticians among the 2,500 membership had devised a claim for an 18% pay rise, the implementation of which would cost around £50 million, a sum not a hundred miles away from that required to finance Mr Younger's recent 'rates rescue package'.

A collective statement from the Church of Scotland expressed general sympathy with the teachers but deplored the strike action, though an amended motion had narrowly failed to pass the winning post, wherein the churches would "deplore the situation in which, to pursue a reasonable claim, teachers have found it necessary to resort to strike action".

Meanwhile, Parkland High School prepared for the normal round of activities which constituted the fag-end of its term.

Morris, newly promoted to lighting consultant for the school concert, rapidly discovered the vacuous nature of early promises that such a position merely entailed "switching a couple of spotlights on and off and making sure there's no hanky-panky in the wings".

Before very long, he found himself attending nightly

rehearsals of the quasi-religious musical to be mounted by the school's concert committee. The producer wished him to "get the feel of the show", but Morris's emotions were mainly of concern at the increasingly ambitious special effects he was being asked to produce.

More immediately, however, there were the administrative and organisational difficulties heralded by the advent of Parkland's annual Sports Day. Mr Tod, short of volunteers to drive the school mini-bus that day, had once again located an eager force in Morris Simpson, keen to put his recently acquired driving licence to some use at last . . .

Perhaps the apparent lack of voluntary help in answer to Mr Tod's request could be explained by the fact that many staff seemed to have deserted the common room at lunch-times and intervals for the isolated hideaways of their classrooms; at first, Morris was impressed by what he saw as a sudden change of heart from the likes of Mr Major: at last, he reasoned, they were beginning to take their jobs *seriously* and getting on with some preparation and development work.

It wasn't long, however, before he discovered the *real* explanation behind their collective and self-imposed solitude. It was just approaching the end of the interval one Friday afternoon when he popped into Miss Bowman's room to check up on the video recorder's availability for the last period of the day; unusually for her, his Head of Department seemed most unwilling to admit him to her room. . . .

"Yes, Morris?" she jumped up from a paper-strewn desk and hastened to intercept him at the door: "What can I do for you?"

"Just wanted to borrow the for next period," smiled Morris.

"Certainly, certainly . . . it's, um, in Mr Pringle's room, I think . . . "

"But it's sitting here!" corrected Morris, pointing at the machine and puzzled at Miss Bowman's distracted air. "You were using it yourself last thing this morning."

"What? Oh yes! So it is!" flushed his senior. "Um . . . tell you what, dearie, I'll send a pupil along with it at the beginning of the period and then —"

"No need for that, Miss B," interrupted Morris. "I'll just wheel it over myself." And, so saying, he launched across the room to claim his prize.

"NO!" screeched Miss Bowman. "Um . . . that is, not just now Morris, if you don't, er . . . , mind. I'd really rather . . . "

But it was too late. Miss Bowman's voice tailed into embarrassed silence as Morris caught sight of the bulky manilla envelopes, postmarked 'Dalkeith', and the partly corrected examination papers which were the substance of Miss Bowman's guilty secret.

To his horror, Morris realised that — contrary to all regulations — some of his colleagues were actually bringing their SCE marking into school! Having been teaching for less than three years himself, Morris was of course unable to apply for a position as an SCE marker, and it infuriated him to see the flagrant breaches of propriety being committed by those members of staff who were supposedly blessed with a greater degree of experience than himself.

His disappointment in Miss Bowman, nevertheless, was as nothing compared to the resentment he felt towards Mr Major when he entered the staffroom next Monday morning . . .

Monday 1st June

Arrived in school to find a "please-take" which asked me to "supervise Class 3P in the continued absence of Mr Major", a somewhat irksome request given that it was for my only free period of the day.

Upon launching further enquiries into the nature of Mr Major's illness, I confess to being a deal shaken by Mr Pringle's explanation that our elderly colleague was probably, as he put it, "marking time . . . " More detailed disclosures revealed that Mr Major is particularly susceptible to severe bouts of influenza and/or gastric disorder at or around this period every year, which illnesses — according to Mr Pringle — are not entirely unconnected with his position as a marker for the Scottish Examination Board.

Pringle sounded fairly convincing, but I really think he's displaying a severe lack of trust in Major's professionalism.

Tuesday 2nd June

Spent much of the day endeavouring to avoid the headmaster, whose unpredictable fits of temper have become increasingly frequent of late. Mr Major, who returned to school this morning looking suspiciously healthy, informed me that the head's nervousness is probably attributable to the impending arrival of the HMI Report on the school.

Wednesday 3rd June

Staff members who yesterday felt that the headmaster could not be more awkward or intractable were proved severely mistaken this morning subsequent to the arrival of the long dreaded Report from! The staffroom was abuzz with comment on the aforementioned document when I popped in for morning break, but it was lunch time before I could lay hands on a copy.

Having thoughtfully scanned its every word I found myself at a loss to understand what all the fuss was about and confided in Mr Major that it all seemed innocuous enough to me.

"Of course it is!" he snapped. "That's why the head's so upset. It's an *appalling* report, Simpson."

"But they haven't actually said anything *bad* about us." I retorted.

"No," he explained patiently. "I'm afraid that's the whole point. They haven't said anything bad and they haven't said anything good *either*. It's a classic example of the whitewash report: apparently harmless but with venom spitting out from between every line. It'll be obvious," he said, glancing sharply at me, "to anyone with the slightest degree of intelligence that this is a real hatchet job."

I requested further elucidation so he accompanied me to a corner of the staffroom and went through the Report "blow by blow" as he put it.

He explained, for example, that when the Report said that the school was under "a long established leadership which maintained a low profile", all it meant was that the headmaster is never seen out of his study except to put in demands for morning coffee and afternoon tea while the rest of the staff get on with running the school.

Furthermore, Major elaborated, it seems that when HMI

recommend "the encouragement of inter-departmental liaison within the curriculum", it means they've noticed that none of the staff ever speak to each other — unless it's in the pub at four o'clock.

Comments relating to the "enthusiasm engendered by the physical education department" simply mean, according to Major, that "our kids are very good at running round a gym", which I had to admit was an observation hardly likely to enhance our academic reputation.

Most startling to *my* ears, however, was Major's snorted response when I pointed out the clause which noted the "relaxed and open style of discipline within the school". Apparently this was the most damning indictment of all, as Mr Pringle was quick to confirm: "Oh, use your brain, Simpson, for heaven's sake," he interrupted. "All *that's* doing is telling the rest of the world what everyone here already knows — since they did away with the belt the little buggers can shout, scream and rave all day if they want, and there's not a damned thing anyone can do about it!"

Why can't these people say what they *mean*?

Thursday 4th June

Eliot, one of the Fourth Year's most unpleasant boys, has been banned from appearing in the end-of-term concert, *Jesus Christ Superstar*. For some unfathomable reason he had been cast as one of the 12 disciples, but was caught during rehearsals last night endeavouring to seduce Mary Magdalene in the orchestra pit.

I have offered to take him under my wing and let him help with the stage lighting; I'm not very fond of the boy, but I think he could respond well to being granted a measure of responsibility.

Friday 5th June

Sports Day. A disastrous conclusion to the week.

Having been entrusted with the task of returning to school with five sets of hurdles and seven giggling adolescents in the back of the school mini-bus, it was hardly surprising that I missed the correct turning on the way back from the sports field.

70

More distressing, however, was my misjudgement of the distance between the school gate-post and the side of the bus; having peremptorily dismissed young Maxwell's offer "tae guide ye in,surr", it was all the more galling to hear the unmistakeable rasp of metal against concrete. Once stopped, attempts to reverse away from the post served only to enlarge the ugly dent which had appeared above the off-side wheel arch, and Maxwell's observation that he had thought I was "cuttin' it a wee bit fine" did nothing to improve my temper. I issued a punishment exercise and ordered them to evacuate the bus immediately.

It being already 3-15, the headmaster had of course gone home, so I was unable to report the incident and will have to spend my entire week-end anticipating his reaction.

A fitting end to the day was provided by the sight of Sinnot, a Third Year boy whose intolerable behaviour has temporarily deprived him of the right to receive education at the ratepayer's expense. He has not, apparently, been overly distressed to be ostracized from the classroom in this fashion; indeed, he spends the larger part of each day sitting on the school wall, smoking copious quanitities of cigarettres, in which position I discovered him at 4 o'clock.

As I strode past this acne-ravaged example of British Youth on my way to the bus stop, the young hooligan had the temerity to wave an over-friendly paw in my direction, which salutation he swiftly conjoined with the greeting: "Afternoon, Surr. Nice day furr a suspension, eh?"

I pursed my lips and passed by on the other side.

I think I am beginning to hate children.

June 1985

Despite Mr Pringle's perceptive interpretation of HMI's report, Mr Douglas need never have lost any sleep over its outcome. Although the veiled criticisms contained within such reports are nearly always obvious to readers of an educational bent, so to speak, it remains true that few other people have much interest in the voluminous tracts, other than the parents whose offspring attend the school concerned.

In point of fact, little emphasis is placed on such reports when parents are forming their assessment of a school, anyway; by far the most popular source of information in this sphere is 'local knowledge': all parents will know somebody who knows somebody who: (a) is a cleaner at the school; (b) is a friend of the school janitor or; (c) works in the school kitchens. Far greater reliance can be placed upon *these* people's assessments of the school than on any mountain of excessive verbiage contained within an official report. *These* are the people who can tell you about the amount of litter in the corridors, about what happens when the kids step out of line and at what time the teachers' cars leave the car-park at night: on such weighty evidence is judgement balanced.

Insofar as the HMI report is of any value to parents in formulating an honest assessment of their children's school, most get their information from a condensed version published in the local press; these 'potted summaries' will normally confine their attentions to the report's introductory blurb on catchment area, a quick run-down of last session's examination results, and a snappy *precis* of the report's final paragraphs.

The first and second of these sections merely state information which is already *known* to parents, whilst the third is usually an attempt to dish out medals to everybody — even if the army's in tatters — by making as many positive remarks as possible. Lifting such doubtful tributes as "making a worthwhile effort in difficult circumstances" or "much potentially effective teaching to be developed" out of the report's entire context ensures that parents hear what they want to hear and abandon the paper little the wiser.

One sight the Inspectorate would not be present to witness at

Parkland High would be the annual, end-of-term prize-giving ceremony, and that was probably just as well, for prize-givings were — in the egalitarian 'eighties — certainly not *de rigeur* among top-flight educationists.

To brandish and encourage open competition in academic excellence was perceived as being contrary to the spirit of comprehensive education in general — and grade related criteria in particular. Nevertheless, Parkland High persistently contrived to mount a large scale annual prize-giving, in direct contravention of wishes expressed by the division's education officers.

Many staff members — Mr Major, in particular — felt similarly disenchanted with the ceremony, though it had often been remarked that his displeasure was more closely related to the perennial quest for an easier life than to any sound educational arguments. The annual struggle to maintain discipline along a thin blue line of whispering First Years, while a distinguished Old Boy held sway with tales of former glories, understandably held little attraction for him.

Perhaps as a result of his rather distressing accident with the school mini-bus, it soon transpired that Morris's services were not required to assist with the prize-giving organisation. This was something of a relief to our young hero, for his every waking moment was now concerned with the illuminatory demands of *Jesus Christ Superstar*.

One positive aspect which had emerged from his electrical involvement with the concert had been the emergence of the boy Eliot as something of a technical expert. For all his disciplinary faults, the lad seemed to have a natural affinity for circuitry, voltage and wattage ratings, and his surprisingly astute theatrical mind had soon devised a lighting scheme in accordance with the aesthetic demands of the show's producer.

Unfortunately, his lamentable absence of self-control was still making itself manifest in the other, curriculum based, areas of school life.

Mr Pickup and Eliot did not get on.

On three previous occasions, Eliot had been threatened with exclusion from Pickup's school trip to Austria, but Pickup had always been prevailed upon by the Depute Head to 'give the boy another chance'; in the penultimate week of term, however, the two had found grounds for disagreement once more, and Pickup had halted his lesson on irrigation methods until the boy saw fit to apologise for the appalling vulgarity with which he had just interrupted the proceedings.

Far from expressing regret, Eliot had responded with an extremely vivid selection of personal insults, with the result that a torrid shouting match was approaching its zenith as Morris popped his nose into Pickup's classroom to ask for the boy's assistance with a little matter concerning a freznel spotlight.

Fortunately, Mr Pickup had his back to the door, so Morris remained unnoticed.

"And if you think I'm taking you within *spitting* distance of the continent, Eliot," Pickup was screaming, "you can think again! I've got better things to do with my time than look after verminous beasts!"

"Ye canny stoap me comin', surr," Eliot was bawling in return: "It's a' peyed fur, an' ye canny stoap me!"

"That's what *you* think, sonny," grimaced Pickup. "If you so much as *step* on that Cross-Channel Ferry, it'll be over my dead body!"

Just a shade louder than intended, the unfortunate miscreant muttered the words which sprang, unbidden, to his lips: "Aye — an' that could be arranged . . . "

"*WHAT* did you say?" bellowed Pickup. "What was that? Did I hear you right, boy, for believe you me . . . "

But Eliot had had enough. "Ach, bugger off!" he scowled, before signalling the end of discussion by retreating, without permission, to his seat in the back row.

Just in time, Morris jumped smartly out of the doorway, two seconds prior to Mr Pickup's furious departure in search of Mr Tod. Blind to anything but his own indignation, he failed to notice Morris in the corridor outside, and brushed past him in a mounting fit of incredulous wrath.

Once more opting for discretion, Morris hurried away to repair the spotlight himself. Conscious of the, forthcoming necessity for Mr Douglas to write his first year's probationary report, he wished to remain as far removed from controversy as possible .

His fervent wish was that Eliot's little outburst would not preclude his helping out at the concert. Although nominally in charge of the lighting console, Morris was only too aware that the dramatic effects lined up for the musical were completely dependent upon Eliot's good offices, and he wasn't happy to anticipate the headmaster's reaction if anything went wrong. Conversely, however, he looked forward to a substantial degree of kudos should the lighting prove as spectacular as he hoped, and on this somewhat flimsy optimism he founded his hopes for a satisfactory conclusion to the academic year.

Monday 24th June

Last week of my first session! Mr Pickup of Geography has withdrawn from the fourth-year trip to the Continent. Despite being "second in command" of the excursion, he dropped this bombshell at morning break after the depute rector had once again refused to exclude Eliot from the party. Eliot, you may remember, is the boy with the appalling disciplinary record, to whom I have given a "second chance" by allowing him to assist with stage lighting for the school production of *Jesus Christ Superstar* this week.

Pickup was still fuming about the business at lunch-time and did not take kindly to my suggestion that Eliot's anti-social behaviour might be due to his poor home circumstances.

"Look, Simpson," he growled between clenched teeth, "I don't care if the little savage lives in a cave and eats sawdust for tea: no pupil's telling *me* to bugger off and getting away with it — or at least that's what I thought until Tod stuck his oar in!"

When I confessed my support of Mr Tod's view that exclusion from the continental trip might only serve to heighten Eliot's regressive tendencies, Pickup practically exploded and, to cut a long story short, insisted on putting *my* name down to accompany the party instead of him; indeed, I have been practically forced to take responsibility for Eliot's behaviour abroad, not a charge I shall relish.

Despite the inconvenience of cancelling my proposed summer cycling tour of Midlothian, however, I can't help but think my position as deputy leader of a school trip abroad will look fairly impressive on any future applications for promotion.

Tuesday 25th June

I feel a tinge of concern over the headmaster's report concerning my first probationary year, which he is due to discuss with me tomorrow.

On reflection, however, perhaps it will not be so bad. Over the past nine months the head has struck me as being an honest, but fair, man, and he *is* due to retire at the end of the week, so may feel kindly enough disposed to overlook any of my minor indiscretions in the year past.

Wednesday 26th June

A stormy meeting with the headmaster this morning which fulfilled my worst fears over the contents of my Probationer's Report.

We had a very long session wherein he asked me to sign an indictment which claimed, among other things, that I was "lacking in disciplinary control" and "well-intentioned in curricular reform". I told him that I considered the latter to be damnation with faint praise and the former to be positively insulting. Furthermore, I informed him that I refused to append my signature to a report which seemed vindictive and narrow-minded in the extreme!

I think he will have admired me for standing up to him, though this didn't seem terribly apparent as I left his study.

Thursday 27th June

An appalling day.

Tomorrow's final performance of *Jesus Christ Superstar* has had to be cancelled, and blame has been apportioned to me in an prime example of what I can only describe as a witch-hunt.

The trouble arose because of a minor conflagration which ultimately blacked out the concluding scenes of tonight's performance. Eliot had assured me, in no uncertain terms, that his lighting plot for the crucifixion scene would in no way overload the electrical capabilities of our somewhat dilapidated lighting board.

Apparently, however, the use of multi-coloured stroboscopic effects in conjunction with 18 spotlights and a neon-filled cyclorama was enough to set the lighting board aflame and the concluding scenes of the musical were slightly marred by the panic stricken attempts of a heavily costumed Roman centurion to extinguish the flames with a nearby extinguisher.

Fortunately Mr Major, who was backstage, managed to restore order to the situation by dousing the blaze before the arrival of the fire brigade, but the upshot of it all was an enforced black-out of the entire hall for several minutes and the near-complete destruction of the school's stage-lighting system.

The headmaster, whose guests for the evening included five local councillors and the divisional education officer, was not impressed, and he singled me out once the last of the audience had departed.

"Well, Mr Simpson," he began. "I think we could safely concede that we have just witnessed a fairly spectacular — and fitting — conclusion to your first session with us."

I said nothing as he ushered me into his study.

"I am perfectly prepared to admit," he continued, his voice awash with sarcasm, "that there may indeed be a Biblical precedent for the onset of darkness at the crucifixion of Our Lord, but I hardly feel that a school play necessitates such a faithful representation of the events on that day. Or perhaps you disagree?"

His expression became hard, angry, bitter.

"I don't have long to go as headmaster of this school, Simpson," he rounded on me, "but there are two more duties I still intend to perform with regard to your future here. The first is to relieve you of any subsequent position containing the *slightest* degree of responsibility for the end of term concert . . . " He paused.

"And the second?" I inquired meekly.

With a slow and deliberate flourish the headmaster withdrew my probationary report from the top drawer of his mahogany desk and laid it down in front of me. Removing the cap from his fountain pen, he tested the nib on a sheet of blotting paper, and, with a meaningful glare, thrust it into my hand.

Heaviness in my heart, I signed the wretched document and handed it back.

"Thank you, Mr Simpson," he oozed, the relish obvious in his voice. "That will be all."

The last bus having long since departed, I set out on the long walk home, my dreams of future promotion disappearing into the cold night air.

Friday 29th June

Prize-giving day.

Mr Major refused to attend and remained in his classroom for the duration of the proceedings, reading his morning paper. He claimed that his protest was aimed at highlighting the incompatibility of using grade related criteria to assess pupils so that no one was compared to anyone else and *then* compiling an Order of Merit and awarding prizes at the end of the day. I confess to a certain ideological sympathy with his viewpoint but suspect the motives behind his absence may have been less than genuine.

Anyway I maintained a decidedly low profile after last night's debacle, and endeavoured to keep out of everybody's way at the subsequent retiral party for the headmaster. I am consoled by the expectation that our new head is likely to give me a fairer hearing than this one, whose departure I am not distressed to witness.

My most immediate concern, however, is the continental trip and its associated preparations. We set off for Germany next week and Eliot is in my party. I am a little apprehensive.

July-August 1985

Morris, of course, had every reason to be apprehensive about his suddenly arranged visit to the Continent, for a trip abroad with twenty-five adolescents can be a harrowing experience.

Society tends to have a slightly ambivalent attitude towards its concept of "the school trip": the days have long since gone when a nature outing to the local zoo would suffice as an adequate 'treat' for the end of term, and an entire industry has developed which caters for the lucrative market of ferrying willing teenagers and their teachers across the continent.

The advantages for the tour companies are obvious: guaranteed numbers, registered child minders in attendance, and a clientele whose chances of framing successful complaints against sub-standard accommodation and semi-poisonous food are negligible — the kids don't know the difference, and the teachers aren't paying for it, anyway . . .

Indeed, for onlookers outwith the education system, these continental jaunts are considered nothing less then a 'freebie', a chance for teachers to get even more out of their abnormally long holidays than their stay-at-home colleagues, and it has to be admitted that many teachers have been able to sample countries and customs in this manner which would otherwise have been far beyond the resources of their pockets.

Nevertheless, it has also to be recorded that many of the 'stay-at-home colleagues' have already *been* on this type of 'holiday' — and have sworn never to go again — and that the parents of the holiday customers are usually lost in eternal gratitude that *somebody* will give them peace for a fortnight! The parents of fifteen-year-olds are normally among the first people to agree that accompanying their children on holiday is not necessarily the sinecure it may appear, for the troubles which can arise are manifold, and tend to be in direct proportion to the average age of the group.

In this respect, the pupils of Parkland High were no different to any other party of teenagers, eager to develop a sense of healthy curiosity about matters more normally associated with adult pastimes.

Apprehension about the coming weeks apart, however,

Morris was not distressed to have completed his first year in teaching. His probationary report was a source of keen disappointment, of course, and the lofty idealism with which he had entered the profession some ten months previous was beginning to show undoubted signs of strain.

It was a strain which, inevitably, affected the entire education system: a Lothian study into the condition of school buildings had revealed, in June, that £27 million was required for essential repairs and maintenance, yet the entire repair and maintenance budget for educational buildings in the region amounted to only a third of that sum! Meanwhile a continental study revealed that British teachers were the third lowest paid in the Report's catchment area of twelve western nations.

Lest anyone forget the struggle, then, *EIS* targeting had been resumed for a brief, pre-holiday reminder in 114 secondary schools from June 13th when, in immediate terms, most teachers were looking forward to the summer break; in the long term, a dismal second year of fighting lay ahead.

For Morris, the only ray of light amidst the encroaching gloom was the increasingly unrealistic hope of a promoted post to boost his monthly pay packet. Promotion at such an early career stage would have been unusual in one of such tender years, but Morris had not forgotten Alan Dickson's helpful remarks about Brownie points: the more he put *into* school life, he reasoned, the greater were his chances of getting something *out* of school life. Perhaps results would not be immediate but eventually, he felt certain, what had been sown would be reaped.

Ironically enough, such were his thoughts as he finished packing a holiday suitcase in readiness for the Austrian trip which began on the 8th of July.

Monday 8th July

An early rise to pick up Miss Honeypot of the PE department, my co-leader on the Fourth Year Continental trip. We had an overnight ferry connection to make before crossing Holland and Germany on our way to Austria: I must say I'm looking forward to what is essentially a free holiday, and one which may even improve my promotion prospects!

The coach trip to Hull was somewhat marred by the unpleasantness of our courier/driver, a rough-featured gorilla of a man called Bert, who insisted on smoking pungent untipped cigarettes for the duration of the journey.

I decided to make an early demonstration of my overall authority by pointing out that he was setting a poor example to the pupils and politely requesting him to extinguish the said cigarettes immediately.

He took the wind out of my sails to a certain extent by drawing attention to the fact that the back seat of the coach bore more than passing resemblance to an opium den, a fact which had hitherto escaped my notice.

Needless to say, Eliot and three of his cronies were found to be responsible, despite having been warned that any pupil discovered smoking on our holiday would face the severest punishment. I confiscated three packets of king-size immediately and repeated the threat as forcefully as possible.

Tuesday 9th July

Slept through most of Holland in a vain attempt to recover from the traumatic experience of endeavouring to maintain order among a party of 38 adolescents set loose on a sea crossing. I *had* hoped Miss Honeypot would assist in ensuring that none of our party strayed into the numerous duty-free bars on board the ferry, but she and Bert seemed to have struck up something of a friendship, and I saw very little of her after 9 pm.

Her presence would, I am sure, have been of some value in the attempts to relieve seventeen cases of violent seasickness which presented themselves at my cabin door between the hours of 1 and 5 am; indeed, Eliot seemed subject to a particularly nasty bout, and for once I found myself experiencing sympathy for the boy — a sympathy which quickly evaporated when it became evident that his nausea was almost solely attributable to the large quantity of alcohol he had managed to consume behind my back!

The arrival at our overnight stop was slightly later than stated on our itinerary; Bert seems to be having a spot of trouble with the clutch on the bus. It makes the most appalling grinding noises whenever he changes gear, but Bert assures me that it has just been replaced and is merely "bedding in", as he puts it.

Wednesday 10th July

An extra day in Germany, enforced by the complete failure of the clutch. Bert — whose mechanical knowledge seems limited to an awareness of the dip-stick's location — was content to relax in a local bistro for most of the afternoon, along with Miss Honeypot, instead of attempting to effect a temporary repair.

The local garage eventually arrived and demanded exorbitant sums of money before they would *even* look at the damned thing, never mind fix it!

Our subsequent decision to allow the pupils a "free evening" proved sadly misguided: only three girls turned up at the Scrabble championship which I had taken some pains to organize, and it soon become apparent that Eliot's notion of "freedom" did not coincide with my own.

To explain, I had just succeeded in placing my second seven-letter word of the evening when the hotel door burst open and three armed German policemen frogmarched Eliot into the centre of the room!

It transpired that the stupid boy's craving for nicotine had induced an attempt to obtain replacement cigarettes and, not content with breaking our own party's rules, he had conspired to flout German law as well: the little hooligan had been round practically every cigarette machine in town and filled them all with five pence pieces instead of Deutschmark coins in a flagrant attempt to defraud the proprietors!

A terse and fraught bilingual discussion ensued, but the police eventually agreed to accept my word that he was indeed part of our group. I have threatened to send him home.

Thursday 11th July

Eventual arrival at our resort was somewhat marred by the discovery of a mix-up over the accommodation arrangements. The hotel manager has kindly offered me the use of a studio couch in the lounge bar after closing time, but I cannot pretend to be enthusiastic about the situation.

Friday 12th July

The holiday is rapidly turning into a disaster of epic proportions. Austrian hotels appear to have extremely flexible licensing laws, as my 3 am retiral last night will testify. Unsurprisingly, I slept through most of our afternoon coach trip to see a glacier.

Again, much of my time *this* evening had to be spent mounting a strict campaign of solitary vigilance on the hotel's bar doors, a task made more trying than it might otherwise have been by the continued absence of Bert and Miss Honeypot.

I remonstrated strongly upon their return from a local discotheque at five minutes to midnight, but Miss Honeypot laughed the whole episode off: "Oh, don't be such a wet blanket, Mr Simpson," she cooed, with what I presume she imagines to be an alluring smile: "If you can't enjoy yourself on holiday, where *can* you enjoy yourself?"

I tried to remind her of our joint responsibility as leaders of a school trip, but she had already turned on her heel to join our nomadic friend at the bar. Speechless, I resumed my position at the door.

I shall file a strong complaint with the deputy headmaster when we get home.

I must say the holiday has been a disappointment to me. The only mitigating factor to date was the arrest of Eliot by the Austrian police early this evening after overdoing things at a schnapps-tasting session. He looks likely to be detained in custody for the furation of our stay here.

We return to Scotland next week. Perhaps I should resign before the next session begins . . . .

August-September 1985

The chances of Morris Simpson offering his resignation were small, for where else could he go, what else could he do? Nevertheless, the fact that it was a possibility which even crossed his mind was indicative of the increasing tension to which he felt subject.

In fact, Eliot's removal from daily involvement had ensured that what was left of the continental trip had passed without major inconvenience or disaster, though Morris did promise himself — on more than one occasion — that he would never, ever again allow himself to be lumbered — and lumbered was the word — with the task of being chaperone to a co-educational group of fifteen-year-olds who found themselves eleven hundred miles from the restrictions of parental management.

The nightly 'bedroom patrols' had, alas, proved to be a traumatic and revealing experience for a man who felt a moral responsibility to ensure that the yearning appetites of adolescence remain unsatisfied and the bounds of propriety remain uncrossed. Sadly, the pupils were not the only ones subject to the torments of fleshly lust, and it was a source of profound professional regret to him that Miss Honeypot contrived to set such a poor example to the boys and girls in her charge; it was indeed difficult to ignore the highly pitched giggling which emanated from Room 54 in the early hours of the morning, mingling — as it did — with the rough untutored tones of Bert, eager to promote yet another loud and dubious declaration of undying affection.

Morris's concern that the children might be unduly influenced by such goings-on was only matched by his disgust at the lengthy silences which invariably followed such expressions of tender endearment. Never a vindictive person, he nevertheless looked forward to a confidential word in Mr Tod's ear once the party had returned to native shores.

For those members of staff who had remained at home, however, the month of July had been marked by the announcement, on July 18th, of that year's "Top People's Pay Award". In a pronouncement cunningly timed to coincide with a period when most people could reasonably be expected to take little interest in political matters, a government-funded pay rise was granted to the top civil servants in the land.

Sir David Hancock, for example, Permanent Secretary at the Department of Education and Science, was to receive a salary boost of 32%, an increase which moved him up to the £60,000 per annum bracket. In what must have been a singularly *un*independent pay review, it had also been decreed that increases ranging up to 46% be granted to other top earners, including judges and generals.

Incredulous reaction to the appallingly tactless nature of such rises was obscured by an officialese smokescreen about "having to pay top rates for the top people". The natural corollary in the world of education seems never to have presented itself, and the summer weeks dragged on with little apparent prospect of an improved offer for teachers, despite Allan Stewart's piously offered hope that July and August offered a "window of opportunity".

In fact, moves *were* afoot, but much of them furtive, and all of them behind closed doors. The management side of the *SJNC* had spent some time assembling a package of pay increases acceptable to both unions and government, but their balloon of anticipation was, to coin a phrase, decisively pricked by the Secretary of State's surprise announcement of a "Teacher's Pay Offer" on August 5th.

At first sight, it was an interesting proposal: an extra fifty million pounds *had* been made available, but the mathematically ingenious hitch was that this sum had to be added to teachers' salary increases over *four years*.

Morris was still naive enough to agree with Mr Younger's own assessment of the offer as "unique in its generosity"; what he failed to recognise, however, was that this offer of 10% over four years — or five, if Mr Younger's earlier statement that no money was available for a 1985 increase was still to be believed — amounted to something in the region of 2% per annum, to be added to whatever eventual salary rise was hammered out at the annual bargaining rammies.

It wasn't really good enough, and the *EIS/SSTA* leaderships had little hesitation in refusing to an agreement for something which was akin to a mess of potage. A subsequent survey carried out by the TESS suggested that 98.75% of responding teachers supported that decision.

To return to the more particular events at Parkland High School, August's first fortnight witnessed the staff girding up their professorial loins for a return to the fray. They still awaited news of a replacement headmaster, and staffroom gossip had it that an appointment was unlikely before the October break, an administrative nicety which would, so the story went, save a tidy sum of money down at Salaries; more immediately, a newly created post for an extra Assistant Head Teacher (Curriculum) was on offer to educational bounty hunters . . .

It was a one of Morris's most cherished desires that the new appointments and consequent refocusing of the school's management structure would prove advantageous to his prospects. He had never really had a chance to *prove* himself, he felt, and looked forward to a deal more sympathy than he had ever received from the old regime.

His most pressing concern at the commencement of that Autumn's term, however, was a keen anxiety to discover the exam results of his *SCE* candidates; sadly, a glimpse at his diary for the week beginning 2nd September reveals these hopes — like so many before and so many after — remained forlorn.

Monday 2nd September

A stormy departmental meeting this morning wherein Miss Bowman, our head of department, spent much time stressing the school's collective disappointment over last session's SCE results in O Grade English.

Without mentioning me by name, I was led to suspect that she found my section's results particularly distressing; admittedly, only two out of 28 presented had achieved a pass of any description (one at D grade and one at E), but I felt she was being unneccessarily critical. I have always believed that education is about so much *more* than examination passes.

Tuesday 3rd September

Sought out Mr Tod, the depute head, this morning in an effort to broach my concern over Miss Bowman's implied criticism of me at yesterday's meeting. His proved an unsympathetic ear.

"*Implied* criticism?" he queried instantly. "I would have hoped she'd be more straighforward than that, Simpson."

My hopes of a fair hearing vanished swiftly as Mr Tod chose to bring up the matter of the fourth year Continental trip last month before launching a vitriolic attack on my professional integrity.

"In addition to being responsible for the most disastrously abortive school trip abroad in living memory," he seethed, "it can have escaped few people's notice that pupils under your charge last session had the worst collection of examination failures in the entire region, never mind this school alone! Wait until the newspapers get their hands on our league performance. We'll be *crucified* in the local press!"

I endeavoured to introduce my point about education's wider aspects, but Mr Tod brooked no interference.

"Exams aren't everything, eh? They are in this town, sonny — and don't you forget it. Why don't you try getting the little toe-rags to do some *work* now and again? Every time I walked past your room last year it looked more like a congealed rugby scrum than a class of O Grade candidates!"

I launched upon an explanation of the communicative benefits to be derived from improvised drama sessions but was, once again, forcefully interrupted.

"And another thing. Why don't you get rid of those damned silly groups you seem so keen to organize in your classroom and get the little buggers all sitting in straight rows? At least you'd be able to see when one of them falls asleep then."

I decided that a delineation of the socially advantageous results likely to arise from group teaching would not be appreciated, so maintained a dignified silence and waited for his ire to subside.

"One final point, Simpson," he concluded. "The video recorder and television will *not* be available for your use this session."

"But Mr Tod!" I cried out: "My media studies course!"

"Forget it, Simpson," he hissed venomously. "Once you've proved you can teach properly, *then* we'll let you wheel in the telly for a film show and a rest every fortnight."

I could hardly believe my ears. To think that our depute head's knowledge of media studies should extend to "a film show and a rest every fortnight" speaks volumes for his awareness of current educational trends. The man is a fool. I shall take my case above him once our new headmaster is appointed.

Wednesday 4th September

More suddenly than anyone had expected, the school learned the identity of our new headmaster in this morning's staff bulletin. Mr Ross is due to take up his position next month, and I look forward to an easier relationship with him than with his predecessor, a man whose dislike of me had grown to unreasonable proportions by the time he had left.

Thursday 5th September

Interviews for the new assistant headteacher's post take place today. Apparently Mr Major, our department's assistant principal and a man with whom I've crossed swords on a number of previous occasions, has applied. I would think he has virtually no chance of getting it: he really isn't very up to date with recent developments and rumour has it that his knowledge of educational technology is limited to the use of coloured chalk for board work!

Friday 6th September

Mr Major got the job! The announcement was made at the morning interval today and I could not find it within myself to hide my astonishment when discussing the matter with Mr Pickup of Geography.

"But it's an appalling choice, Pickup," I spluttered over my lunchtime sandwiches. "I know I don't get on very well with him, but it's not just that."

"Oh?" Pickup glanced inquiringly at me.

"No. It's the man himself, and the consequences for the school. His teaching methods are *completely* out of date, he has even less discipline in class than *I* do, and he seems to have no interest in the pupils whatsoever!"

"Exactly," confirmed Pickup. "That's why he got the job . . . "

"Pardon?"

"That's why he got the job, Simpson. Use your brain lad. On all three counts he's ideal material for an AHT's post. Of course we all *know* he couldn't control a group of 10-year-olds, let alone a class of 30 adolescents. Now he's been promoted he won't need to go anywhere near the little sods: he can spend all his time dishing out please-takes, mounting curricular reforms and raising funds for the school mini-bus. It gets *him out of the way* . . ."

"But that's appalling —"

"Maybe so. But it's effective. Anyway, he was always front-runner *whatever* he said at the interview."

"Him? Why?"

"Well, he and the new head are in the same lodge," Pickup continued. "Don't tell me you didn't know *that?*"

"The same lodge? You don't mean that both Major and Mr Ross are . . . ?"

"Of course, Simpson. The old pals' act. Secret passwords. Fancy aprons. *The Tufty Club*," he whispered fiercely, tapping the edge of his nose and squinting over the coffee table at me: "Masons. . . ." Dumbfounded by Pickup's bombshell and its implications for myself, I retired to an empty classroom to ponder my next move.

Perhaps I should apply for a transfer.

September — October 1985

To be fair to the teaching profession, masonic influence and nepotism would appear to be somewhat limited within the groves of Academe, and Parkland was perhaps unusual in possessing two such initiates. More popular by far, among Headteachers in particular, is membership of the ubiquitous Rotary Club.

Not a man to do anything by halves, Mr Ross — as will eventually transpire — was a fully paid-up, card-carrying member of both. It has to be said, however, that his enthusiasm for the arguably noble ideals set in motion by both movements' founders was on a fairly equal footing with his appreciation of a good lunch and the chance to get back to school at about 3 o'clock in the afternoon — most especially on corridor duty days — under the guise of having had to "attend an important meeting".

Such discoveries were all before Morris, of course, but his hopes for a more fruitful career had begun to vanish from the moment he had learned of the close friendship which existed between his new Head and Mr Major.

Disappearing almost as swiftly were the larger-scale hopes of an early settlement to the year-old dispute. September saw the *SJNC* Management Committee's initiative formally rejected despite the fact that it had posited a 15% pay increase to be phased over three years. The already mentioned *TESS* opinion poll, officially *EIS*-ignored, unofficially endorsed by membership response, suggested that the majority of respondants would settle for little less than 20% — now — and John Pollock, caught in the embarrassing position of having 'blacked' a survey which came out almost wholeheartedly in his support, agreed that it *did* present an accurate representation of teachers' hardening attitudes.

By the end of September, a euphemistically titled "return to previously sensitive areas" (targeted strike action, by any other name) had been introduced, affecting 1500 teachers and 30,000 pupils for three days of each week. The *TESS* survey confirmed that 80% of all unions' membership were in full support of their leaderships' respective campaigns, a sobering indication of solidarity in a punch-drunk system of education.

On the 16th of October, in what was subsequently viewed as a knock-out blow, and in one of the largest ballot returns in its 138 year history, the *EIS* announced that a majority of 87% had voted to boycott all procedures related to the coming session's SCE examinations. To take, momentarily, a retrospective view of the pay campaign, this was the moment, for many teachers, when they finally got the message across that they meant business. Apart from the relentless water-drip of targeted action it was, in effect, the ultimate weapon — and one which was deployed with the utmost reluctance, if all accounts are to be believed. Nevertheless, it is perhaps not too fanciful to notice the beginnings of a slight but perceptible alteration in Government approach subsequent to the October ballot.

But this is to anticipate. For Mr Ross, it was an awkward moment to take up his new post, and he felt something akin to the leading player whose first appearance is halfway through Act Three, but he set to with a will and determined to make an early impression upon his new colleagues. Those few members of staff — like Morris — who were eager for curricular initiatives and the implementation of a new school ethos were soon to have their worst fears confirmed, for it rapidly became apparent that Mr Ross, like his predecessor, had a healthy cynicism for such educational tinkering. For Mr Ross, a ten-minute assembly and a morning staff-bulletin amounted to a whole-school policy — or as good as — and he still had an undisguised antipathy towards the notion of mixed-ability classes, preferring instead to separate (in his terms) "the sheep from the goats and give the smart kids a chance . . . ". Unusual in one who had reached the rectorial pinnacle, he had the interests of staff at heart, and his first task of note was to set up a social committee to ensure that their recreational demands were fully satisfied. Appropriately enough, Mr Pickup was entrusted with its Convenorship, and a regular staff cheese-and-wine party was soon announced for the last Thursday of each month.

For his own part, Mr Ross set about the time-consuming task of interviewing each member of staff on an individual basis, from which meetings he soon expected to gauge his new school's strengths — and weaknesses. It was a meeting which Morris viewed with some apprehension: he only hoped that the head would have had time to acquaint himself fully with the mitigating circumstances which had contributed so much towards his inauspicious start in the teaching world.

In a frantic attempt to impress, he threw himself fully into the preparation of his class grades for the October Assessments. It was probably just as well that his union had by now advised him, in line with his colleagues, to withdraw *completely* from all extra-curricular activities: Miss Bowman's new scheme of assessment had much to commend it, but had proved to be more demanding of his time than he could ever have envisaged.

Inevitably, not everyone in Parkland found themselves so busy. .

Monday 15th October

Mr Pickup, who used to run the school chess club, has initiated a regular lunch-time bridge session in the staffroom; he claims that the extra-curricular ban is the "best thing since Houghton" but, sadly, I find myself unable to take advantage of our newly-acquired free time.

Despite the curricular boycott on new development work for Standard Grade, I am increasingly snowed under with paperwork. At present, all of my energies are directed towards the marking of comprehension assessment items from both of my first-year classes, a task which has effectively removed all of my preparation time; additionally, I have 62 oral fluency assessments to conclude with the second year before the end of next week.

I despair of finding time for everything.

Tuesday 16th October

Decided to approach Mr Major, my ex-departmental colleague and newly-promoted AHT for some advice on my workload this morning. After all, he *is* AHT in charge of curricular development and, given the present industrial situation, would appear to be doing precious little to earn his responsibility allowance!

My quest proved illuminating, to say the least.

"Reading comprehension assessments?" he queried, his brows knitted. "You don't mean *Interpretations*, do you?" he continued.

"Well, yes," I confessed, surprised at Major's utilization of such old-fashioned terminology. "I've got 59 of them to mark and hand back before Friday, in preparation for this term's assessment grades. It's a very time-consuming job, you know. "

"But you don't mean you mark them *yourself*, do you?" he inquired.

I nodded assent.

"Good God, Simpson, what on earth d'you do *that* for? Get the little buggers to swap papers with their neighbours and let them mark each *other's*."

"But, Mr Major," I interrupted, "that's hardly very fair. I mean to say, it's wide open to cheating, and these marks go towards their final grades. I've *never* allowed them to mark each other's papers."

"And *I've* never allowed them to do anything else!" he declaimed. "Cheating? So what? You don't think anyone pays any *attention* to these grades, do you? After all, their end-of-term reports are so full of bumf and educational jargon that any parent who ploughs through every single subject report deserves a medal for bravery and stamina, never mind finding time to complain about cheating!"

Uncertain of my ground, I stared emptily at him.

"No, no, Simpson," he continued, warming to his theme, "just let them mark their own. When it comes time to write their reports, simply make up the grades as you go along. How many grades do you have to give to each pupil, anyway?" he inquired.

"Fourteen," I admitted.

"There you are, then!" he declared triumphantly. "Nobody expects you to knock your pan out on that score. Most of the little sods'll get a majority of C grades, a fair proportion of B's, and as long as you shove in a couple of A's here and there no one's going to take the slightest bit of notice. If you think they're capable of stringing two or three sentences together at a time, simply bump up the A grade ratio."

I *had* always thought that criterion-referenced assessment required much closer attention to detail than Mr Major implies, but I must admit that his scheme has much to commend it. . . .

Wednesday 17th October

An appointment this morning with Mr Ross, our new headmaster.

Well warned of his Masonic connections by Mr Pickup, I resolved to refrain from venturing any opinions on this post-pubescent version of the Boys' Brigade. Nevertheless, I think I failed to impress him to any great degree; the meeting commenced rather shakily when I offered a firm handshake, hoping to indicate thereby my strength of character. Unfortunately, he failed to respond, except with an extremely limp grasp and the surreptitious trailing of his index finger across my palm.

Unaware of how best to react, I stammered an introduction, but he appeared to have lost interest in whatever I was saying and spent much of the appointment sorting distractedly through a bundle of education department circulars before falling to a detailed examination of his briefcase and its contents.

The only concrete information to emerge from our interview was that he had discussed my distressing probationary report from last year *most* fully with Miss Bowman, my head of department. He also expressed grave concern over my O Grade section's examination results last session.

I suspect that he's not going to be terribly well-disposed towards the problems of a second-year probationer.

Thursday 18th October

Entered the staffroom at lunch-time to discover a veritable hive of activity and interest centred on the noticeboard: virtually all of the unpromoted staff-members were squeezed together around what turned out to be the latest issue of the "Job-Sheet", a regional notification of currently available posts affording extra responsibility — and pay.

Little thinking it worth my while to consult one of these wretched documents, I turned sadly in the direction of my locker and located a rather stale cheese sandwich.

Friday 19th October

I have decided to apply for promotion!

Having dismissed the prospects of advancement out of hand yesterday lunchtime, I crept back to the staffroom at five past four, when the staffroom was deserted, and noticed that the position of assistant principal teacher in St Ainsley's, one of our neighbouring schools, is vacant. I realize that such an application may be slightly premature, but at least the interview will be good experience and perhaps I can get Mr Ross to write my reference before he finds out too much about me.

Mentioned my plan to Mr Pickup just before the afternoon interval: strangely enough, he seemed to think I was joking, but when I assured him of my commitment to the application and asked for his honest appraisal of my chances, he straightened his face and muttered something about stranger things having happened at sea.

Mr Pickup has a wry sense of humour.

Despite my request for strictest confidentiality in the matter, I was dismayed to witness him scurrying in the direction of the staffroom when the bell rang, a broad grin creasing his face. More embarrassing still, I could not help but hear an outburst of raucous and uproarious laughter emerge from behind the closed door some 30 seconds subsequent to his entry.

This collective reaction of my so-called colleagues has made me more determined than ever to advance my career.

I'll show them.

October — November 1985

It was yet another illustration of Morris Simpson's "green unknowing youth" that he should apply for a promoted post before the conclusion of his second probationary year. The era of early promotions had been — and gone — in the 1970's, when local authorities, keen to inject fresh vigour and new ideas, had visibly encouraged the appointments of relatively young Principal Teachers, Assistant Heads and, in some cases, Headmasters. Laudable in its aims, this policy nevertheless had the inevitable effect of creating a large and constipated bottleneck in the 1980's promotion structure, replete with all of the frustrations which constipation can bring.

And then, with regard to the particular job at which Morris had tilted his javelin, there was also the question of his religious suitability. Oh, of course he had read the footnote on the 'Job Sheet' which informed that candidates for this post would require to "satisfy the Roman Catholic authorities" with regard to their suitability, but he had failed to grasp its full implications. An innocent abroad, he had naively assumed this to be a reference to good character and a belief in the Christian faith; it was Mr Pickup who later informed him — albeit somewhat cynically — that these two considerations were often the *last* to be taken into account when making such an appointment!

Again, however, this is to anticipate. For the present, the battle raged without relief as Sir Keith Joseph disclosed his not-so-secret wish to see education authorities suing teachers who caused disruption and — in passing reference to the local difficulty north of Carlisle — added his hopes that English teachers would not "sink so low" as to hit examinations.

Encouragement enough — if encouragement were needed — for the *EIS* to launch a planned escalation of action which would leave much of the country on a two-day educational week by Christmas. At last, it was felt, the Government had actually acknowledged there was a dispute in Scotland — and it was a different one to England's.

Yet even within Scotland there were disputes within the dispute, as it were, for teachers in Strathclyde and Lothian were *still* embroiled in a row over 'three-day cover': a genuine sense of grievance existed on both sides, for the teachers felt it grossly unfair that neither authority seemed willing to provide replacement staff when lengthy absence occurred among one of their number; the authorities, for their part, plead poverty, unavailability of supply teachers and distress at the lack of compromise, lack of give and take being displayed by their employees. Perhaps they had forgotten that, at base, a lack of compromise was really what the larger dispute was all about.

Meanwhile, the larger dispute was still in good health, for one of the largest 'walk-outs' in its history occurred on 8th November, when 1000 *EIS* members departed the country by British Rail to join their *NUT* colleagues at a London rally. In terms of its £50,000 cost, the day-trip represented fairly good value for money, for it once again brought the Scottish dispute to English eyes in a graphic statement of Pictish determination to see the whole sorry saga through to the end — complete with pipes and drums!

Battles are not only won by the generals, however, and Morris soon found himself part of that small infantry which had been formed to distribute information sheets about teachers' pay and conditions to households in areas which surrounded the school. The October Assessments having been completed, at least it made a change from marking jotters of a winter evening, but, as we shall discover, he found the entire exercise somewhat discouraging.

Not only that, but he was rapidly forming a worse opinion of Mr Ross than of his predecessor! He could understand the man's desire to court popularity, but not at the expense of the profession's dignity. He couldn't help but wonder if the man was really *sound*.

Monday 25th November

Any hopes of improvement for the educational ethos of the school have been dashed since our new headmaster has seen fit to donate a pool table to the staff common-room. The vast proportion of male staff now spend their lunch-hours emulating boorish snooker players or throwing darts at a somewhat infantile caricature of George Younger on the staffroom notice board.

I complained to Mr Pickup about the purchase of the pool table, an action I can only perceive as a gross misuse of educational resources, but he countered with the accusation that staff were merely catching up with the senior pupils, whose common-rooms had been kitted out with such tables, as well as pinball machines, some three years ago.

It seems a petty argument to me. . . .

Tuesday 26th November

I'm on the short leet for promotion!

Despite the amused reactions of my colleagues last month, I decided to apply for the post of assistant principal teacher of English at St Ainsley's High, one of our consortium schools. The news came through today that I've to attend for interview at the regional education offices next month. I expect it to be a fairly rigorous session so will swot up on as many different reports as possible in the immediate future.

Strange to say, my Geographical colleague, Mr Pickup, appeared to be unimpressed by the news.

"Fair enough, Simpson," was the only congratulatory remark he could bring himself to utter, "but don't expect too much. You're only in there to make up the numbers y'know."

"Come, come Mr Pickup," I smiled condescendingly. "You're not going to tell me that *this* job's rigged in the same preposterous way as you claimed the new assistant head's was?"

"No, no Simpson — at least, not in *quite* the same way. . . . "

"By which you mean . . . ?"

"Well — let's put it this way: far be it from me to even *hint* at the possibility of religious bias in the eventual appointment, but I'd be very interested to learn the — um — spiritual aspirations of the other candidates on the short leet. I'd *suspect* you're in there in case the Equal Opportunities Commision comes charging over the mountainside in a blaze of egalitarian zeal."

"Oh, Mr Pickup!" I exclaimed laughingly. "You don't honestly believe, in this day and age, that just because I've applied for a post at a Roman Catholic school — "

"I'm afraid I do, Simpson," he confided, "and I'm afraid it's something you'll find out soon enough for yourself. In the meantime, I think you'll discover that there's something of an 'unofficial short-leet' and *you* won't be on it. *You kick with the wrong foot, son,*" he hissed ominously.

Shocked into initial silence by these revelations, I eventually brought myself round to tell Pickup that I'd never heard such a ridiculous proposition in my life. Religious bias indeed!

Wednesday 27th November

Mr Pringle's union, which has the largest representation on the staff, had organized some leaflet distribution tonight in an effort to inform parents and residents of the severe professional dissatisfaction behind the current industrial dispute; despite being a member of a more traditionally moderate union, I expressed a desire to join the entourage in a gesture of brotherly solidarity. Sadly, the evening turned into something of a farce owing to our collectively-belated departure from the hostelry whence distribution arrangements were to be launched.

Those of us who actually got round to posting our material through letter-boxes were dismayed to encounter very little positive support from the public: indeed, aside from persuading one irate parent that I wasn't a "raging Communist with over-long holidays and a part-time working day", my longest conversation was with a lady who refused to be convinced that I wasn't a representative from *Reader's Digest*.

Sometimes I wonder if we're getting our message across to the public.

Thursday 28th November

A "please-take" for Mr Dunbar of the Maths Department, who has been off all week. Mr Tod, the depute rector, agreed that I would be losing some of my already minimal non-contact time, but urged that he would be willing to make up the deficit if I could "just help him out this once".

Somewhat reluctantly, therefore, I found myself in charge of 2B(3), a lower-stream collection of reprobate under-achievers. Thinking to introduce some inter-departmental liaison, I set them some straightforward tasks of mental arithmetic which required the compilation and costing of an average household's weekly shopping requirements.

Much to my consternation, however, it appears that the Mathematics Department is in the habit of distributing pocket calculators for even the simplest of exercises, without which machines these children refused to attempt the exercise.

What to they *teach* them in Maths these days?

Friday 29th November

An almighty row has erupted over the business of yesterday's "please-take"! Because Mr Dunbar had been off for three days, his absence should apparently have been covered by a supply teacher; unfortunately, the region's staffing department have been unable to provide such cover, and Pringle got to hear of my involvement.

Having emerged from a stormy encounter with Mr Tod this morning, he called a union meeting for lunch-time and subsequently announced three days of industrial action next week.

Attempts to explain my own position were confounded by the fact that those involved in the forthcoming strike have refused to acknowledge my existence since the meeting; even Mr Pickup turned sharply on his heel when confronted with my enquiries in the corridor this afternoon. So much for brotherly solidarity!

Despite Pickup's earlier warnings about the interview, I have set my sights firmly on promotion and an early farewell to the ill-assorted collection of child-minders who seem to staff this school with little but their own self-interest at heart. Things might be easier when I am in a position of some authority.

November —
December 1985

Before his temporary banishment to Coventry, Morris might
have been well advised to give credence to Andrew Pickup's
warnings, for there are few sights more pathetic than hope about
to be crushed. Undeterred, however, he set about interview
preparations with an enthusiasm which had been almost
forgotten since college days. Nightly visits to the local Resource
Centre allowed him to amass an impressive bundle of recent
educational reports, all of them devoured in a voracious quest
for self-improvement. Time after time he mentally prepared
answers to the questions which were *bound* to come up: his views
on mixed-ability teaching, the use of the school library as a
resource centre, the merits of block timetabling,
interdisciplinary liaison and co-operative teaching. Let them
hurl what they may — Morris Simpson was ready and waiting!

Perhaps it was just as well that he couldn't hear the
conversation which took place between Mr Ross and Mr Major
on the morning of Monday 9th December.

John Ross had spent a worrying two days mulling over the
draft edition of his new school's prospectus, and something was
still bothering him. It *had* been a good idea, he felt sure, to hand
the responsibility over to Bob Major, for the poor bugger didn't
have much else to do with his time these days. Nevertheless,
Bob seemed to have lost his touch for the odd dose of sparkle,
and the prospectus was an important document. Indeed, he
found it hard to remember how schools had ever managed
without them. On reflection, it had probably been the "Parents'
Charter" which had given the impetus: once you allowed kids to
vote with their feet, you *needed* to have a glossy baggage of self-
promotion to drag in the customers, but it was a source of some
concern that the document should hit the right note.

And this wouldn't do.

"I'm sorry, Bob, but there it is. I'm afraid I just find it awfully
dull."

"Well of *course* it's dull!" snorted Major. "I'm not exactly
Jeffrey Archer and this isn't exactly Butlins' Holiday Camp —

though I sometimes wonder about the latter. You can't make a silk purse, y'know, John."

"Oh, I know that, Bob, but for heaven's sake, we *are* trying to bump up the roll next year before they close down the Classics Department. We're hardly going to get the AB 1's and 2's if you suggest that Parkland High's most exciting educational innovation in recent months has been the introduction of cafeteria-style service in the Dining Hall, now are we?"

"Well, I suppose not, but — "

"And another thing. What's this about 'streamed classes throughout the school'?"

"Well, that's what we've got, isn't it?" Major defended himself.

John Ross muttered a silent invocation before launching a strained but patient explanation: "*I* know that, Bob. *You* know that. But the Divisional Education Officer doesn't know it! And if he ever finds out I'm still shunting the thickies together in the vain hope that the rest of the kids'll actually *learn* something, he'll have my balls strung up from the top floor rafters before you can say 'Standard Grade'!

"What you need," he continued emphatically, "is a nice wee blurb about stretching *all* pupils to their maximum potential whilst ensuring that the individual needs of those requiring remediation — sorry, those pupils with learning difficulties — are fully catered for within mainstream education. We need some *jargon* in there, Bob."

"Oh, come on, John," protested his friend of long standing: "You know I can't write that kind of garbage. You'll be wanting something in about interdisciplinary liaison next, not to mention a challenging personal hygiene scheme and an actively anti-racist stance within the hidden curriculum!"

"Well, actually," mused Mr Ross, "that's more or less exactly what I *do* want, old boy . . . ; but I see what you mean: it's not really your style, is it?"

"No it's not, and I can't for any sake imagine who you'll get in here that's . . . hang about, though," Bob Major interrupted himself. "Why not ask . . . "

"Of course!" shouted the Headmaster. "Why didn't *I* think of it? I presume you're thinking what I'm thinking, Bob?"

"The Young Pretender?"

"Yes! The little twat in your Department, eh? He's got all that kind of educational crap spewing out of every orifice, if I remember rightly. That's our man. Take him the draft copy and tell him to tart it up so that the D.E.O.'s impressed with the number of buzz words we've got in , but so that any prospective parent knows *exactly* what we're doing here — trying to educate their kids in spite of everything!"

"Wilco, Headmaster!" laughed Major. "Mind you, he's up to his armpits with interview preparation at present. Maybe I should leave it till after Christmas?"

"Like Hell you will! I want that prospectus ready before the hols, and a library copy sent to the Education Offices on 20th December: that way, it'll get shoved into a drawer before the Xmas party, and forgotten about by New Year, so with a bit of luck, no-one'll examine it too closely."

"Brilliant. And Simpson?"

No chance, anyway. I had a word with McKean at St Ainsley's last week just in case he suffered a mental aberration and gave the boy the job."

"And . . . ?"

"Oh, you know Tom McKean: just laughed, thanked me for the tip, and said not to worry — the first we'd know of whoever gets *that* job would be when we saw a puff of white smoke emerging from the school chimney. 'Nuff said?"

"I think so, Headmaster," Bob Major winked a bushy eye, before gathering the draft beneath the voluminous folds of his gown and hurrying in search of our young hero. . . .

Thus it was that Morris found himself burdened with yet another area of (unpaid) responsibility, but he shouldered it manfully, ironically delighted at what he reckoned to be an extremely broad hint about his chances for filling a post with more responsibility. . . .

As Morris prepared, the *EIS* reviewed: it had been a successful conclusion to the term, for a National Strike on 5th December had received almost unanimous support once more: 10,000 teachers had turned up at a rally held in George Square, Glasgow, and many thousand others at equivalent rallies in Edinburgh, Aberdeen, Inverness and Dundee.

Guarded support was even forthcoming from Strathclyde's Director of Education: in an unusually candid memorandum distributed after a further £5 million cut was announced in the Region's Education Budget for the forthcoming year, Edward

Miller was moved to note: "the fact that important progress has been made in a number of educational fields in Strathclyde is due to the commitment of staff whose loyalty we strain with increased demands without additional resources."

At the end of November, Mrs Thatcher herself had begun to take a personal interest in the campaign, at least to the extent of meeting her Scottish Secretary of State and other senior ministers to discuss the dispute and even — *mirabile dictu* — accepting, in a House of Commons reply on 26th November, that Scottish teachers would require an increase of 8% to keep up with cost of living increases. Bob Beattie, of the *EIS*, had an understandably alternative mathematical argument to suggest that 19.5% was a more accurate figure, but these were minor quibbles: the straw to which Scottish teachers attached their hopes over Christmas '85 was the fact that, at last, senior members of the Government had actually begun to notice, and respond to, their pressure — and not before time.

Though not unaware of these events, we have already learned that Morris was somewhat preoccupied with matters of a more direct personal relevance; one, final, blow came with the discovery that the extra-curricular ban had been extended to the previously sacrosanct Christmas parties which were traditionally arranged for the pupils. This was a source of some concern.

Monday 16th December

A trying week ahead; my interview for an assistant principal teacher's post takes place on Wednesday morning and much of my spare time is devoted to catching up on the numerous working party reports with which I *must* be familiar if I am going to stand any chance of getting the job.

At the same time, however, everyday school life is proving tiresomely awkward, owing to further staffroom intransigence and consequent bitterness over the cancellation of this year's Christmas parties. Personally I feel it to be a disgraceful reflection on the profession that we can't bring ourselves to spread a little Christmas good cheer among our adolescent charges; in fact, I stated as much publicly at the inter-union meetings held last month to discuss the matter.

However, Miss Honeypot of the PE department was the lone voice in agreement, and I couldn't help wondering whether *her* enthusiasm for staff/pupil functions was entirely unconnected with a recently developed interest in McLaren, a rather gangly member of the sixth year . . . .

Pringle, the union rep, did not endear himself to our new headmaster, Mr Ross, by informing him of the staff's refusal to supervise the dances, and I must say it pleased me to note the head's comment regarding the unreliability of judging public opinion from the emotion-laden atmosphere of a union meeting, where convictions are so easily swayed. He told Pringle that in such circumstances teachers were voting in a peculiar psychological arena, and I couldn't help but indicate my agreement during what turned out to be a fairly torrid session with Mr Pickup this afternoon.

"And anyway, Mr Pickup!" I emphasised, "what good has it done you? The seniors are *still* holding a party, except they're organising it themselves and it's going to be held in the lounge bar of the *Pig and Whistle*. You realize there'll be under-age drinking there, don't you? And where shall we — their moral guardians — be on *that* night?"

"Well, I don't know about you Simpson," he rejoined, "but I'll be popping along there myself and hoping one of them buys me a drink."

"What? But you don't mean . . . ? You can't mean to tell me that you actually *condone* their illicit . . . ".

"Not particularly," he interrupted, "but let's face it, that's where most of them spend their Saturday nights anyway, so why shouldn't I go along and join in the fun this time? All that matters is we've shown the buggers at the top that we're not prepared to jump around and organize their end-of-term party games any more without due recompense. What I do with my own time after school is my concern entirely — and *don't you forget it!*" he spat in a fierce declamation which signalled the end of our discussion.

I remained silent, but was secretly disgusted to hear of such goings-on. I begin to suspect that rumours of his involvement with Amanda Torrance of the sixth year may have some degree of truth after all. Aside from anything else, his selfish approach to the senior dance omits entirely the problem of the juniors, for whom no such alternative arrangements are possible.

Tuesday 17th December

Interview preparations.

Little time to write except in noting my decision to throw an end-of-term party for my first year class on Friday afternoon as some form of recompense for the sorry conclusion to their first term in secondary school.

Early to bed.

Wednesday 18th December

I didn't get the job . . .

Despite lengthy and arduous preparation for what I assumed would be a thorough grilling on educational theory, developmental practices and departmental organization, I am horrified to report the travesty of a discussion which passed for a job interview.

Having assumed a potential interview length of at least 40 minutes in mental rehearsals, it was a salutary blow to recognize that I left the room some eight minutes subsequent to my entry! The questions, practically all of which emanated from my prospective new headmaster, seemed almost exclusively concerned with my willingness to run his ruddy school football team as well as take charge of the staff social committee.

Not only this, but he chose to bring up the matter of my first year's probationary report and hinted darkly that my application for a promoted post in his school smacked, at best, of ingenuous optimism and at worst, bare-faced cheek!

It was with little surprise, then, that I learned of my failure this afternoon, but I was touched by the heartfelt commiserations of Messrs Pringle and Pickup, who seemed genuinely disappointed to learn that I would not be moving on to pastures new. Perhaps this isn't such a bad place to teach after all.

Thursday 19th December

I have decided to throw myself more fully into class preparation and marking next term, having calculated that honest-to-goodness integrity in the everyday matters of actually *teaching* might ultimately bring about recognition in the form of promotion. If it does not, I shall not worry unduly. Pickup tells me that I'm rationalising failure, but I've told him he's a cynic!

Some concern has been voiced over Mr Major, our newly promoted assistant headteacher: the staff are worried about his recently-acquired habit of patrolling the school complete with a personal stereo cassette player, its attendant headphones affixed firmly to his ears. Mr Pringle sympathises and sees it as providing an ideal method of escape from the strains and tension of what he chooses to call Major's "daily round and common tasks".

Perhaps so, but to my mind it doesn't seem to set a very good example.

Friday 20th December

The afternoon party which I organized for my first year class turned, I am afraid, into something of a debacle.

Having provided a small collection of decorations, paper hats, balloons, orange juice and eats at my own expense, I was pleased to see things running smoothly for the first 15 minutes until Marshall, a small blonde-haired child with behavioural problems, expressed a desire to invite "a few pals" from 1F, being taught next door by Miss Fraser. It being, after all, the last day of term, I saw little objection to extending the festive goodwill a little further and readily consented.

Events snowballed, however, and it seemed little time before a mass entourage of what appeared to be the entire population of the first year, the only group to record near-perfect attendance today, had formed a seething mass of humanity in my already overcrowded classroom. Mr Major, fortunately patrolling the corridors to the strains of Handel's *Messiah*, was unable to hear the commotion — but not so the depute head, Mr Tod. . . .

He stormed into my room at ten past three demanding to know "what the bloody hell's going on here", only to interrupt the trajectory of a well-filled portion of gateau being hurled across the room at that moment by Marshall.

Silence ensued.

Having cleansed the accumulation of chocolate filling from his glasses and the spatterings of cream from his waistcoat, he issued an immediate instruction of dispersal, and, the room having been evacuated, glared fiercely in my direction.

"Far be it from me to spoil the festive celebrations, Mr Simpson," he enunciated between clenched teeth, "but perhaps you wouldn't mind reporting to my office at 9 o'clock on the first day of term next year, when we can discuss this little . . . um . . . incident more fully . . . "

Misgivings in my heart, I viewed his departure into the corridor with some degree of apprehension and slowly, dejectedly, began to take down the paper chains from around my blackboard. I wonder if it's too late to send him a Christmas card?

December 1985 —
January 1986

The second Christmas of the pay campaign was not very different to the first — only worse. The liquidity problems experienced in the previous eighteen months could only be exacerbated by the consumer demands of a Christmas period which saw new spending records set — but not by teachers, for whom the monthly arrival of the Barclaycard demand was becoming more and more the source of hysterical laughter rather than serious concern.

If subsequent events were to prove anything of a guide, however, the Christmas period must also have been something of a strain on those members of Mrs Thatcher's cabinet involved in what was to become known as 'The Westland Crisis'. On Thursday, January 9th, Michael Heseltine stormed out of a Downing Street cabinet meeting, removed a metaphorical handkerchief which the Prime Minister had been attempting to thrust into his mouth, and consequently removed himself from office as Secretary of State for Defence. The parliamentary game of musical chairs which he thus set in motion saw George Younger ensconced in his place, at last in a position to to abandon his Highland Clearances — as the extended run-down of Scottish industry had come to be known — and move his pencil sharpeners to a new desk in Whitehall, from which he would now budget the country's defence.

His thoughts on off-loading the albatross of Scottish affairs from around his neck were not fully recorded, only his distinct sense of honour at being asked to take up such an important new position; his replacement at St Andrew's House, Malcolm Rifkind, had a similarly nebulous statement about his pleasure at finding himself thus promoted from the Foreign Office, though he must have recognised the enormity of the problems which lay before him.

But the arrival of a new face in St Andrew's House gave cause for renewed hope to many. What chance now, the staffrooms queried, of an early settlement? Sensibly non-committal at such an early stage of his new career, Mr Rifkind gave every indication that he at least wanted to get *something* done about the teachers; in what had been practically his last act as Secretary of State for Scotland, his predecessor had, in the first week of January, formally rejected the initiative presented to him in September by the Scottish Churches, perhaps a suitably negative conclusion to his many ill-fated attempts to achieve a settlement in the past eighteen months.

Not, in all honesty, that he hadn't *wanted* to solve it, but — to use a cricketing analogy — if the captain of the team insists you bat until close of play, then bat until close of play you must — especially when the captain could be as unforgiving as Mrs Thatcher. Whether the shrewd and astute qualities of Mr Rifkind would register any greater success remained to be seen, but he certainly recognised the gravity of a situation where the *EIS* had just announced their plans for January and February, plans which involved hitting every school in Scotland during the succeeding eight weeks: 250 secondary schools would be "seriously affected", and similarly hit would be 1,800 of the 2,400 primaries.

But Mr Rifkind had other unfinished tasks to consider, other messes to clear up: the steel works at Gartcosh seemed certain to close, and the consequent threat to *BSC*'s plant at Ravenscraig would have to be hotly denied, at least until after the next election; another rates row loomed, this time concerning an eventual introduction of the Government's long-promised ratings reform, a package intended to please everybody and — as is the nature of these things — managing to please nobody. In the three card trick which formed the new Secretary of State's immediate hand, the only possibility of playing a trump would have to be a short sharp solution to the teachers' pay dispute.

Of course, the teachers were not the only group experiencing problems of finance: as will have become abundantly clear in the course of this narrative, the entire education system was still experiencing threats to its continued viability and, in a novel interpretation of the self-help philosophy so beloved of the Government, Henry Dutch, Strathclyde's head of public relations, fostered the notion that there was money to be made in jotters — or, to be more precise, in jotter covers. Gone were the days when a list of socially instructive "Do's" and "Dont's" would appear on the back page of every school child's jotter;

gone were the days of principals' independence and individuality in purchasing jotters from Andrew Whyte, Holmes McDougall or the grandly titled Grant Educational Company, jotters overflowing with pages, and jotters which would stand up to the rigours of the heavy-handed thirteen-year olds who were going to use them; in their place came the ubiquitous standard issue from Central Stores: pale green ranks of identikit jotters, most of them enleafed with something which approximated to recycled toilet paper, all of them designed to last for approximately three periods of work before the clarion call arose: "Surr! Ah need a new joattur!"

But the best thing of all about these jotters, it suddenly dawned upon Mr Dutch, was that they had *space*! Space on the front, space on the back, space on the inside covers, space, in fact, all over the place, and none of it being *used*! In a sweeping fit of entrepreneurial zeal, he had the newspapers informed that — from the beginning of the next session — advertisements would be allowed, nay, actively encouraged, to fill out the broad expanses of Strathclyde school jotters. Nothing tacky, you understand — no South African conglomerates or contraceptive manufactureres, just a broad selection of kosher ads from the 'safely neutral' (*sic*) firms who sell insurance and breakfast food, as well as the more obvious input from the anti-smoking, anti-drug and anti-anything lobbies. At two and a quarter thousand pounds per 500,000 exercise books, it looked like a good deal for the advertisers but, more importantly, it was expected to rake in £50,000 per annum to Strathclyde's hard pressed educational coffers. Education authorities elsewhere took note . . . .

The only complication, it appeared, would arise when teachers insisted on ensuring that pupils protected school property adequately by covering *all* books and jotters, for the adverts would be thus obscured. Mr Ross had thought of this, however, and a memorandum was issued to ensure that his solution was brought to the staff's attention. Sadly, it had slipped Morris's attention.

To be fair to him, this was hardly surprising, for he had been subject to increasingly stringent demands upon his time in the first weeks of term: although his senior pupils were excused regular classes because of their preliminary examinations, he was once again bowed under with marking, this time for the January Assessments. Despite the sterling efforts he had made in assisting Mr Major with the School Prospectus, he found that relations between himself and the newly promoted assistant head were becoming increasingly soured.

This is not even to take into account the obvious disharmony which existed with Mr Tod after the Christmas Party debacle. But then, Mr Tod didn't seem to be terribly popular with *anyone* at that particular time . . . .

Monday 27th January

A furious argument has erupted over supervision of the senior school's preliminary examinations, though I fail to see the logic in Mr Pringle's viewpoint. As our "school representative for Scotland's largest teaching union" as he likes to be known, he has spent the last 18 months of the work-to-rule issuing dictatorial and bloody-minded injuctions concerning the number of pupils he will allow his members to supervise.

Now, in an episode which has been appropriately termed "Mr Tod's Revenge", our illustrious depute head has seen fit to draw up a "revised" supervision list for invigilation during the prelims, in which list he insists upon having one teacher per 33 pupils present within the examination hall.

An otherwise untroubled and relaxing portion of the academic year for most staff has thus become a bone of serious contention: instead of two or three being gathered together for invigilation purposes while everyone else gets on with tidying out their rooms or playing gin rummy in the staffroom, Mr Tod has had the immense satisfaction of viewing eight or nine extremely bored — and frustrated — members of the *EIS* patrolling the serried ranks of adolescence.

Unsurprisingly, the "extra" invigilation duties have been unerringly allocated to members of this union only, and I confess to a deal of secret pleasure at seeing these militants being taken down a peg or two — I'm certainly glad to be in a traditionally-moderate union!

Tuesday 28th January

Arrived at the staffroom notice-board this morning to discover that my *own* name had been added to the revised invigilation list! Seething with resentment over my lost preparation time I sought out Mr Tod, but he assured me that my appearance on the list had nothing whatsoever to do with the unfortunate incident he experienced at the end of last term in attempting to quell the over-exuberance of my classroom party for the first year.

I found difficulty in concealing my scepticism over his denial, but accepted my lot forthwith in the hope that he would reallocate my invigilation period to avoid the necessity of sharing the loathsome task with Mr Major, whose behaviour is becoming a source of serious concern: the man is *still* insistent upon patrolling the shcool accompanied by his ubiquitous Walkman stereo system. He claims that the retreat to privacy which this individual musical companion affords is an ideal vehicle by which he can relieve the tension of his job as assistant head.

Blind to the reasonable strictures of my request, Mr Tod issued a curt refusal so that I found myself some 30 minutes later patrolling the aisles of Higher grade mathematics while the AHT of the school conducted an apparently silent orchestra at the rear of the hall, oblivious to the flagrant cheating being conducted by candidates beneath his very nose!

Wednesday 29th January

I am thinking of lodging a formal complaint against Mr Major.

According to recent guidelines on discipline drawn up by an inter-departmental committee, occasions of misbehaviour arising outwith the school boundaries are *supposed* to be referred, in the first instance, to the AHT responsible.

Having witnessed the disgraceful conduct of Lamont outside the school gates this morning, I took the matter to Mr Major, who is supposed to be responsible for pupils with surnames beginning K-Q.

"And finally, Mr Major," I concluded, having at last persuaded him to remove his ruddy headphones for three consecutive minutes, "the little urchin completed his disgusting abuse of the driver and passengers by actually throwing a *stone* at the bus! It's a miracle nobody was injured, let alone killed!"

"Mmm," mused Major, "And what did you do, Simpson? Discipline has to be enforced by *all* members of staff, you know."

"Oh, of *course* I know that," I snapped irritably, "but when I grabbed a hold of his blazer the little reprobate lurched round and instructed me — I use the boy's own words — to 'get my effin' hands oaff'; after which he told me that he 'wisny in the school yet' and that he could consequently behave as he wished."

Tense with mounting indignation at the recollection of the incident, I awaited Mr Major's response with eager anticipation. Having remained silent for several seconds, however, he eventually chose to mount a detailed investigation into *my* actions!

"Hang on a minute, Simpson," he questioned, "you don't mean to say you actually *touched* this pupil?"

"Of course I do! The boy was committing a criminal offence!"

"Doesn't matter. You got hold of him by the arm?"

"Not at all. I grabbed him by the scruff of the neck before he could do any *more* damage. Surely that's what *any* right-minded teacher would do?"

Again, Mr M remained silent for several seconds but, after much rolling of eyes, he lowered his gaze to the floor and announced that this was really "nothing to do with him", after which pronouncement he reaffixed his headphones to his ears and strolled down the corridor away from me.

"But Mr Major!" I called after him, "surely you're responsible for disciplining the boy?" To my astonishment, my querulous pleas fell on deaf ears and I turned to confront Lamont, surrounded by five of his third year cronies, a broad grin creasing his contemptible face.

"You're in trouble, Lamont," I began, but before I could continue, the arrogant little ruffian had the temerity to interrupt.

"Naw, naw —*sir*," he emphasized. "*You're* in trouble. *Big* trouble. *Ah* know ma rights."

Not trusting myself to reply, I turned on my heel and retreated to the staffroom in a mood of unwholesome bitterness. It infuriates me to think that Major is sitting on a fat responsibility allowance — and doing *nothing* to earn it — while I — despite my devotion to children and their education — have been refused the opportunity of promotion. It's enough to make you leave teaching!

Thursday 30th January

I have issued punishment exercises to my entire first year class and have decided to put them *all* on report. The threat to do so was issued at the beginning of term when I discovered that not *one* of them had covered a class jotter yet. Despite several reminders this week, my jotter inspection this morning revealed that the same situation still obtained.

Marshall, a boy I have had dealings with before, tried to concoct some cock-and-bull story about the guidance staff issuing instructions that no jotters were to be covered henceforth, so I issued him with an extra punishment exercise and told him I'd never heard such arrant nonsense!

Friday 31st January

A summons to Mr Tod's study after assembly this morning. Initial hopes that he intended congratulating me on my strict approach with the first years were soon dissipated.

"Ah, Mr Simpson," he began, pleasantly enough, "just to let you know I've taken 1R *off* report."

"Ah, thank you very much Mr Tod," I rejoined with satisfaction. "I take it you've spoken to them about covering their jotters, then?"

"Indeed, indeed," he concurred. "I presume there's been some misunderstanding along the way, but if you'll just see to it that all the punishments are withdrawn, then I'm sure they'll be quite willing to accept your apologies over the matter."

"Certainly, Mr Tod," I replied, "and perhaps you'd see to it that . . . I beg your pardon?"

"I said I'm sure they'll be willing to accept your apologies over the matter," he repeated grimly, his face hardening.

"My apologies? *My* apologies, Mr Tod?" I stuttered in confusion. "How d'you mean?"

"I mean, Mr Simpson, that you have — and not for the first time — failed to respond to a staff directive issued in the daily bulletin. Don't you *ever* read that bloody news-sheet?"

"Well, normally sir, but I do miss the occasional issue or two and . . . and . . . and which directive do you mean, anyway?" I trembled, confidence awash.

"The one about covering jotters, for God's sake. They've not to *do* it anymore."

"But why ever not? Surely we should be encouraging them to protect *all* school property, especially jotters and textbooks that travel home every day."

"Well in the first place, Simpson, we never allow them to take books home anyway, and in the second we've been told to *stop* them covering jotters, whether they go home or not."

"But *why*?" I pleaded, nonplussed at these latest revelations. "Why on *earth* have they to stop covering their jotters?"

"Because of the bloody *adverts*, you imbecile!" he shouted across the desk. "Ever since the authorities decided to investigate getting adverts on jotters in a feeble attempt to shore up school finances they've been churning out confidential memos urging us to ensure widespread exposure when it actually comes about."

"Widespread exposure?"

"Of course, you young idiot! The fold at Reddy Brek are hardly going to spend 8,000 quid advertising their warm healthy glow on all pupils' jotters if some zealous little prat's going to order his class to cover the damned thing with brown wrapping paper, are they?"

"Well, no, I suppose not, but -"

"Don't give me any buts, Simpson," he cut in. "Just rescind the punishment exercises and make sure the *rest* of your classes know what they're supposed to be doing with their jotters. If you're not sure, perhaps one of the first years will help you out," he concluded with an unnecessary degree of sarcasm.

My bewildered dismissal from his study was issued to the accompaniment of a peremptory reminder concerning my invigilation duties at period two.

My depression upon leaving the room was heightened by the distant appearance of Mr and Mrs Lamont entering the school office in the company of an extremely tall police sergeant. Hurrying to the staffroom, I was able to answer the office's telephone inquiry myself by informing them that invigilation duties would render me unavailable for the remainder of the day. Apparently young Lamont's father is intent upon pursuing a charge of assault and feels he has a very strong case.

Mr Pickup has advised me to see a good lawyer.

February 1986

The month of February really *was* the beginning of the end for Morris Simpson's secondary teaching career. Beset by what he recognised as unwholesome persecution from Mr Tod, he found it difficult to acknowledge that — twice within the space of a week — he had been pilloried for carrying out what should have been the rightful duties of any conscientious teacher. Not only that, but he found himself at the centre of a legal row which made Page 3 of the local press and had him seriously addressing his mind to the possibility of leaving the district. Assured by Mr Pickup, however, that the boy Lamont was merely a living embodiment of original sin, Morris stuck to his guns and decided to fight the assault charge mounted by the family.

Despite the eventual outcome, of which we shall later learn, the entire episode left a bitter taste in his mouth.

Another man who had recently experienced bitterness was a character who has not figured prominently in our story, though no less important a man for that. Many neutral observers of the secondary school hierarchies would, in fact, place him at the top of the somewhat shaky edifice which passes for an efficiently run comprehensive school. He is, of course, the Janitor. For it is not the Headmaster, but the Janitor who holds the keys to the school gates; it is not the Headmaster but the Janitor who starts up the boilers on a cold winter's morning; it is the Janitor who keeps the playground from being turned into a large scale refuse tip, and it is the Janitor who makes sure that, whatever goes on in the school, it can't go on unless he knows about it, and agrees to it! The days of autonomous Rectors may well be over, but the power of the school Jannie remains sacrosanct. He is a man whose friendship it is wise to cultivate, and it is no exaggeration to claim that he is the most important man in the school.

For this reason, if for no other, it had probably been unwise of certain Lanarkshire Headmasters and associated authorities to incur the collective wrath of that District's 360 Jannies in December of 1985. The issue at dispute was the fact that Lanarkshire Janitors were traditionally responsible for the cleansing of school toilets, a task which frequently resembled the purification of the Augean Stables, and a task which — in other districts of Strathclyde — fell to that other noble body of school domestics, the cleaners.

Sporadic shutdowns of schools had already taken place before the situation was inflamed yet further, at the beginning of February, by an extended but related argument about when school boilers should be serviced: the Janitors, for whom the job had long been part of their weekend duties, wanted it — and the accompanying overtime, presumably — kept that way. Some Headteachers begged to differ.

For a tricky few weeks, fourteen Lanarkshire schools went through the tiresome process of opening only if the boilers had been activated long enough before the staff's arrival to ensure that classroom temperatures allowed at least a partial circulation of the bloodstream; even then, many could only remain operational for a couple of hours if the Janitor had chosen to remove heating provision on the instruction of his union.

Although not one of the janitors involved, Andrew Crichton felt a strong sense of affinity towards his oppressed brethren in Lanarkshire, and held a watching brief on events. It would be a foolish man who crossed him but tact and diplomacy were character traits which John Ross had never learned to cultivate.

Meanwhile, Mr Rifkind had been busy. A meeting with representatives from the Scottish Churches on 10th of February had given cause for hope, not least based upon the flexibility which he seemed willing to display. It was a flexibility for which he became renowned, and a quality which was sadly lacking in the five 'hard-line' education authorities in Scotland who had supported February's Bright Idea of docking pay from any teacher complying with results of the Government-Approved-Secret-Ballot to boycott examination procedures. All party support for the idea was essential, however, and the less authoritarian regimes in the country blocked the move — which was probably just as well for the staff at Parkland High . . . .

Monday 24th February

The row over distribution of preliminary examination marks drags into its fifth week and I begin seriously to contemplate the possibility of leaving teaching at the end of my second probationary year.

The "prelim exams" having been held in January, and the marking of same having been complete for the past 21 days, members of the Educational Institute of Scotland are still refusing to make the results known to heads of department in an attempt to block the compilation of Orders of Merit for SCE appeals next autumn. Mr Pringle, the union rep, claims this is in co-operation with his union's policy of *non*-co-operation in exam procedures but Miss Bowman, his and my head of department, has left the union over what is nothing short of a ridiculous abuse of militant power, an observation which I passed on to Pringle himself this morning. What makes the situation all the more pathetic is that individual teachers are quite prepared to let the pupils know their own marks, but are practically forcing them to swear oaths of secrecy before revealing the damn things!

The stupidity and senseless pettiness of such action reached its height this afternoon when Pringle emerged from his higher English class in suspicious mood, only to trip over Miss Bowman, who was kneeling outside the door with clipboard and Biro in hand. His furious accusations to the effect that she was trying to eavesdrop as he checked final scores with the class were strenuously denied by Miss B, but her claims to be searching for a punishment referral sheet which had "gone astray" had something less than a hollow ring of truth about them.

Departmental relations are becoming increasingly strained, what with the consequent rift between Pringle and Miss B, as well as Mr Major's effective withdrawal from any kind of pretence at teaching since his promotion to assistant headteacher.

For my own part, I am unable to rid myself of worries surrounding the impending assault charge being brought against me by the father of Lamont, a reptilian member of the third year, after I inadvertently laid a restraining hand upon the boy's shoulder during a major contravention of discipline outwith the school gates last month. My lawyer is anxious to mount a plea of provocation so that he can fulfill his promise to "screw the little bugger to the floor if the preposterous notion ever reaches court", but my doctor's prescription of sleeping tablets is proving a more effective antidote to mental distress at present.

Tuesday 25th February

Despite having escaped the worst ravages of targeting over the past 19 months, the school's *EIS* members found themselves called out on sudden action this morning.

The school being virtually bereft of pupils, then, those of us in less militant unions received a healthier proportion of free time than usual, an "extra" I anticipated utilising by clearing a back-log of marking and preparation, activities which had to be removed from the A Floor common-room due to the action of our worryingly detached assistant head: Mr Major had at last seen fit to rid himself of the Walkman Stereo he has taken to wearing during corridor patrols and had instead organized a staff game of *Trivial Pursuit!*

My attempts to concentrate were therefore seriously inconvenienced by the puerile shrieks of laughter emanating from the eight other members of staff left in school, laughter which was punctuated — on more than one occasion — by the utterance of some extremely unprofessional oaths!

Despite having made a number of fairly pointed remarks about "chronicles of wasted time", I eventually found it necessary to locate an empty classroom in order that my marking duties could be performed effectively. Major has told me that he's thinking of replacing the annual Scrabble championship held during the SCE examination period with a *Trivial Pursuit* championship.

I despair of the profession.

Wednesday 26th February

Another day of strike action, though neither Pringle's or Major's union were involved. *This* time the school had to be shut down because of janitorial discontent!

Today's "wildcat" action was basically a rekindling of the eight-week-old dispute over the duties of the school janitor. One of the first year pupils had been sick this morning after a particularly vicious incident of bullying in the playground by person or persons unknown: young Marshall, despite having the presence of mind to dash for the nearest toilet when overcome by sudden waves of nausea, unfortunately failed to arrive at any suitable receptacle in time.

The janitor, having been issued with a rectorial injunction to "get rid of that ruddy mess in the first year bogs", promptly disclosed that such tasks were in no way part of his contractual remit and initiated the closedown of the boiler-room, thus rendering the school's heating system inoperative.

It was some time before I learned of such details, of course, for most of my time during period three had been taken up with warding off complaints from 2C, never the most disciplined of groups, about the inhospitable climate of my classroom. Initial emotions of sympathy were soon dissipated, however, for after allowing them the opportunity to bring their duffle coats and scarves into the classroom I was amazed to discover that not one of the boys, and only two of the girls, appeared to have arrived at school with any form of protection against inclement weather.

It seems that the donning of extra layers of clothing beyond the school blazer lays them open — the boys in particular — to a variety of charges, homosexuality among them. I told them that I had never heard such nonsense and proceeded to button up my own duffle coat, wrap a scarf around my neck, and don a furry hat and woolly gloves for good measure!

It was just after Pamela Millstone had drawn my attention to the ice-formation on the inside of the window pane that our depute head put his nose around the door and beckoned me outside. Conscious of the strained relationship existing between Mr Tod and myself at present, I scurried into the corridor immediately, only to be met by a torrent of vitriolic abuse.

"What in God's name d'you think you're doing *now* Simpson?" he hissed bitterly. "You look more like Scott of the fucking Antartic than a secondary school teacher!"

"Maybe so, Mr Tod, but at least I'm keeping warm," I countered indignantly. "If the authorities can't afford to heat the school properly than I think *you* should be grateful that some of us are prepared to remain at our posts in spite of conditions which would -"

"Oh, stop bleating man, for God's sake; nobody's *asking* you to stay at your post — the school was *dismissed* 25 minutes ago after the temperature fell to 40 below . Or didn't you *hear* the headmaster's Tannoy announcement?" he enquired archly.

I decided that my month-old removal of the Tannoy from its wall socket in an attempt to cease the infuriating metallic interruptions to my lessons had better remain a closely-guared secret for the moment and thanked Mr Tod for the information. Having dismissed 2C, I retired to the staffroom, just in time to join a game of *Trivial Pursuit* around the two-bar electric fire.

The headmaster has announced his intentions of starting the boiler himself tomorrow if the janitor refuses to "come to heel" as he puts it. I think he is treading on dangerous ice.

Thursday 27th February

Fortunately, the industrial strife concerning the janitor was resolved by My Tod's valiant offer to clean up the lavatorial chaos, but I couldn't help feeling a sense of vicarious outrage on Pringle's behalf when my second-year registration class informed me of their parents' disgust at two days of strike action being launched by teachers this week. Despite my aversion to his union's vindictive tactics, I saw it as my task to explain the truth of yesterday's events, but found it impossible to make myself heard over repeated and puzzling demands from Burgess of 2C to "dae yur Eskimo imitation surr"; after the seventh such request, I issued a punishment exercise, which seemed to shut him up.

Mr Pickup of Geography, too, had a strange fascination for matters arctic when he spied me at morning break; "Ah, it's Nanouk of the North!" he bellowed across the staffroom, but chose to ignore my gaze of enquiry to sidle over instead and ask about police proceedings in the case of Lamont versus Simpson.

"Well, I haven't heard for certain, yet Mr P," I acknowledged, "but the police are supposed to be finalizing charge details this afternoon and — if it's all to go ahead — I should hear tomorrow."

"Ah — good luck, anyway, Simpson," he urged, clapping my shoulder in a gesture of sympathetic affection, " — good luck."

The increased frequency of such friendly demonstrations since the unfortunate incident had not escaped me, but it was only now that his reasoning became clear . . . .

"And look, son," he continued in confidential vein, "the next time you try something like that, you'd better make sure you're — um — *unobserved*."

"Sorry?"

"Well, let's face it, that little toe-rag's been asking for it since first year: it was only a matter of time before *someone* got their hands on him."

"But Mr Pickup!" I protested in horror, "you're not actually suggesting that I *did -*"

"Suggesting? Me? No, no Simpson," he winked at me. "Never in a hundred years," he smiled knowingly. "But if you *do* try it on with Lamont again," he whispered conspiratorially, "drop round to B43 first and let me know about it. I've wanted to ram that little bastard's head off a wall ever since he walked into my class three years ago and asked who was the 'baldy-heided guy wi' the fat gut'."

Vanity always *was* one of Pickup's weaker points . . .

Friday 28th February

After a sleepless night, I learn that assault charges against me are to be withdrawn! The cheering news arrived at lunch-time, along with the information that Lamont *himself* is to go before the children's panel over the bullying incident last Wednesday.

Nevertheless, the events of the past month have taken their toll: I am becoming more and more convinced that my job is underpaid and undervalued, as well as feeling myself under increasing and intolerable stress.

After long deliberations, therefore, I have come to the conclusion that it is time to hang up my duster and get out of teaching. Pickup, whom I taken into my confidence over the matter, has told me that it's "easier said than done" but has promised to save me the jobs pages from his *Guardian* every day.

For the first time in months, I look forward to the coming term.

March — April 1986

For once, Morris was in good company, for he was not the only person to anticipate Good Things in the forthcoming term, even if his colleagues' rekindled enthusiasm owed more to a Parliamentary announcement than to the prospect of scouring *The Guardian's* job adverts.

On Thursday March 6th, the recently appointed Secretary of State for Scotland gave notice of the Government's intention to set up an independent enquiry into the pay and conditions of Scottish teachers. Possibly as a result of Mr Rifkind's persuasive arguments, possibly as a consequence of flimsy re-election prospects within the next two years, the cabinet had at last been persuaded that some form of concession was required if peace were to return to Scottish schools. An interim pay award of nearly 15%, accommodating 7% from April '85, 2% from January '86, and the rest from April '86, was also slapped on the negotiating table. Strike action, of course, was to cease forthwith.

Initial reaction ranged from the euphoric to the static: there was much talk of a "historic victory", as could have been expected, but some thought it better to examine the finer points of detail pertaining to the statement. Bob Beattie, in what might be accurately described as couthy wisdom, suggested that, compared to Lord Houghton's two line remit, the restrictions placed on the review committee "read like *War and Peace* . . . with more strings to it than a large vest."

Strings or not, the announcement amounted to a remarkable *volte face* from a Government which had spent the last 20 months issuing blunt and repeated refusals to countenance the prospect of allowing an outside body to examine the terms of discontent. Whatever the eventual outcome of the enquiry, it was recognised that the teachers had won concessions where, for example, the miners could not; much of the credit for such a victory — even if its long term effects proved to be Pyrric — would need to be accorded to the streamlined orchestration of the *EIS* campaign, a campaign which financed itself and prepared itself: no "down tools, everyone out, we'll show the buggers" mentality, but a paced, even and relentless campaign of sustained and sustainable action, a campaign which won its media friends almost before it began, and then proceeded to satisfy their copy-hungry demands with a veritable flood of press releases, colour coded for each particular week, shifting the focus of industrial action from one day to the next and thereby ensuring as near-constant coverage as could reasonably be expected: there was little news value in telling a nation that 'teachers were still on strike' on any one day; there *was* value, however, in reporting that 'teachers had moved their strike action to Arbroath, or Stranraer, or wherever.'

The voting in favour of calling a halt to strike action received 90% *(EIS)* and 95% *(SSTA)* support, though the curriculum development and extra curricular boycotts remained in force: at least there would be no Sports Day or Concert worries for Morris *this* year!

Our young hero, in fact, was pleased to hear of his imminent pay rise, but it was, sadly, too little and too late for a reversal of his decision to hunt for another job. He still felt a sense of vocation, a heartfelt desire to work within education, to mould and assist young lives, but the sheer practicalities of everyday school life had proved frustrating beyond belief, and he wanted out of it.

A case in point was the argument which had arisen between himself and Jim Henderson the Classics master — 'Big Caesar' to the pupils. It had come about after Henderson had sought Morris out at the end of a particularly trying day.

"Morris, old chap? Time for a word?"

"Oh, hello Jim," greeted Morris, raising his head from the half-corrected jotter before him. "What can I do for you?"

"Well, it's about wee Julie Smart in the 3rd Year. She . . . "

"Julie? That's a coincidence: it's her jotter I'm marking just now," Morris shook his head at the illiterate scratchings before him. "You know I'm taking her for extra English when she's supposed to be at Gym?" he continued brightly. "She seems to be making a bit of progress, but it's tough going."

"Mmm," pondered the Latin master; " . . . that's actually what I wanted to chat about," he probed: "whether she really *needs* to come for extra English."

"*Needs* to come?" laughed Morris: "I should say it's practically essential if she's going to leave school capable of writing anything other than her own name — and in block capitals at that!" he added. "Why?"

"Look, Morris, I'll be blunt. You know that the 4th and 5th Years are away for their exams at the end of the month? Well, that's going to leave yours truly with a pretty blank timetable, isn't it? I mean, half of my teaching time's taken up with Senior Classes, and . . . "

"That much?" queried Morris. "But I thought there only *were* two candidates for Higher Latin this year?"

"There are," admitted Henderson. "Plus five 'O' Grades, one Higher Greek, and a pair of no-hopers doing Classical Studies."

Morris's voice rose with incredulity: "And that's half your timetable? My goodness, Mr Henderson, I wouldn't mind . . . "

"Look, never mind that just now!" snapped Henderson. "What I've come to see about is shifting young Julie under *my* tender ministrations for the rest of the year: that way, I'll fill in half my blanks till July and the Boss needn't come poking his nose in to see whether I'm earning an honest day's pay."

"Julie Smart?" scoffed Morris. "But the girl can't even speak *English*, never mind Latin, Jim!"

"Oh, never mind about that. She won't get within spitting distance of a subordinate clause: I'll give her a few Classical wordsearches, wheel in that video they all love about the Romans' toilet arrangements and then get her to help me clean up the storecupboard before the end of term. I'm sure she'll enjoy herself."

Morris was nonplussed. "But that won't help her *English*, Jim. And I think she's really beginning to get the hang of things now — she does seem to enjoy her extra periods of language work."

"Bugger the language work! I need a body for my timetable, and Julie Smart's the top candidate: nobody's bothered *what* she does, as long as she stays out of trouble, and the girl herself doesn't know what day of the week it is, never mind what class she's supposed to be in."

"But *I'm* bothered what she does!" protested Morris. "I've taken a personal ineterst in the girl, and the improvement she's shown in the past two months has been just about the only thing I've felt proud about since I came to this place!" His spleen rising in accordance with the volume of his voice, Morris continued, "What makes you think . . . "

"Look, I'm sorry, son," interrupted his elder, "but it's all arranged anyway. You've not really got any choice in the matter, but I figured I'd let you know myself."

"No choice?"

"'Fraid not. Tod's given it the O.K., and that's about the end of it, Simpson."

"Oh, I see. Mr Tod says so?"

"Uh-huh."

His jaw clamped firmly shut, Morris removed the top jotter from his pile and ceremoniously transferred it into the care of the Classics Department.

"Thank-you, Mr Henderson," he strained between pursed lips. "I have some work to be getting on with now . . . if you don't mind," he looked pointedly towards the classroom door.

Jim Henderson took the hint,and Morris was left to ruminate on exactly what constituted an educational priority in the 1980's.

If the only bone of contention Morris felt were over such curricular frustrations, then perhaps he could have survived. As we already know, however, he was assailed by multi-directional slings and arrows, against which he found it impossible to take arms, so the job-hunt increased in ferocity. Although an end-of-April party had been arranged in celebratory expectation of the back-pay's arrival Morris still found that the majority of his own lump sum would just about see him clear of overdraft facilities for the first time since starting teaching. Financial economies would have to be maintained for some time to come, as would be the case in *all* areas of education.

Monday 20th April

My search for a new job continues apace; despite the interim pay award and the announcement of a review to investigate conditions of service, I still find myself determined to locate employment unaccompanied by the petty frustrations of teaching.

A disagreement this morning over photocopier usage is typical of the restrictions imposed upon us by the penny-pinching bureaucracy of remote authority: having spent the best part of my weekend preparing a theme-based unit on the Third World for Class 1R, a dramatic project designed to increase their social awareness, I popped my request for 270 photocopies into the School Office at 10am this morning, only to be met with an unconscionable display of dumb insolence from the administration staff.

"270 copies, Mr Simpson!" choked Mrs Thomson. "By Period 3? You've got to be joking."

"Certainly not, Mrs T.," I countered. "Is there a problem?"

"Not unless you mean Period 3 *next* Monday," she chortled. "C'mon, son," she continued, "you know as well as I do that all material for photocopying has to be sent down at *least* four days in advance. The girls and I just haven't the time to produce fancy wee comics at fifteen minutes notice-"

"Fancy wee — ! Mrs Thomson," I seethed, "perhaps I could explain that."

"And anyway," she declaimed, "we've hardly any paper left."

"But surely we've only just started the new Financial Year? They can't . . . "

"Doesn't matter. Duplication money's been cut by 70%, and I've got just about enough to last until mid-June. If you *really* want this stuff done, you'd be best to try the shop at the corner: they've got a wee machine that — "

Hardly able to control my temper, I found myself on the point of asking her what the hell we had office staff *for* if they weren't able to service staff needs effectively, when I was interrupted by the unctuous tones of an eavesdropper who turned out to be Mr Major, our revered AHT.

"And anyway, Simpson," he butted in, "we can't allow the machines to be taken up by members of the teaching staff who've fallen behind in their preparation time."

Stung into initial silence by his rude interruption, I was mentally composing a suitable response when Major smiled round at our euphemistically titled Administrative Assistant to ask whether she could "just spare a couple of minutes" to dash off 80 copies of a document he required for staff distribution at the morning interval! Needless to say, the wretched virago was suddenly transformed into compliant and willing clerical assistant, eager to assist in whatever way possible, and my querulous tones of protest were swiftly quashed by Major's authoritative explanation.

"And before you start bleating, Simpson," he outlined

firmly, "this is for Administration, and that's different. The paper restrictions only apply to teaching materials . . . "

Speechless with disbelief, I watched Mrs Thomson's smiling countenance as she gently received the paper from Major's outstretched hand, transferred it to the Xerox machine and churned out 80 copies before I could draw breath.

So much for Education.

Tuesday 21st April

Twenty-four hours later than planned, I launched my 3rd World Project with the 1st Year this morning. Having been forced to dispense with the nine page booklet designed to encourage child-centred learning, I was looking forward instead to some good old-fashioned 'chalk and talk' methodology.

Having prepared, then, a trayful of 'junk' food, typical of the average first year child's lunchtime intake, to compare with the barren menu of a starving child in the southern hemisphere, I had it in mind to initiate a number of dramatic improvisations to illustrate the theme of man's inhumanity to man. Discovering my blackboard duster to have been mislaid, however, I found it necessary to borrow one from Miss Fraser next door, an errand which took longer than expected due to the interesting conversation we embarked upon with regard to our forthcoming pay increases.

My eventual return to Class 1R, then, was sadly marred by the discovery that persons unknown among their number had seen fit to remove a round of my lunchtime cheese sandwiches, selflessly loaned for the duration of the lesson as a visual stimulus.

Detailed investigations led to a trail of breadcrumbs and four smirking, chewing twelve-year olds at the back of the class; needless to say, young Marshall was the ringleader, and the little reprobate even had the effrontery to offer me a beef and onion crisp from a packet which I discovered had *also* been filched from my interval snack-box at the front of the room!

My wrath knew no bounds, so I issued four punishment exercises immediately and, although Marshall had the unprecedented cheek to suggest that he "wisnae daen' it", I told him he'd be in *really* serious trouble if he didn't.

Wednesday 22nd April

That little tyke Marshall, the only boy yet to hand in his punishment, arrived at the staffroom door during the morning break with a smug little message to the effect that Mr Tod, our Depute Head, wished to see me as soon as possible, tidings which brought me little joy: at one time I might have expected full backing from the disciplinary hierarchy of the school, but recent events have made me suspicious of anticipating Tod's help in such matters.

Strange to relate, however, he seemed excessively care-worn when I poked a tentative nose around his study door . . . " Oh, Simpson . . . yes . . . um, do come in," he spoke quietly, one weary hand supporting a very furrowed brow. My enquiries after his health elicited the response that he was sickening for a severe bout of influenza and felt something akin to "Death warmed up . . . "

"In the meantime, however," he sighed, "I've received this damned fool of a letter from young Marshall's father," and, in so saying, he handed me a sheet of filthy notepaper covered in near-illegible scrawlings, much of which I was barely able to decipher, but the gist of which roused my temper to hitherto uncharted heights.

Mr Marshall, far from condoning my professional authority, had forbidden his son to perform the punishment issued! The man had the nerve to suggest that *I* was at fault for leaving the offending sandwiches and crisps open to view and then abandoning a class of 30 young adults (sic!), thus laying his son open to the obvious temptation of helping himself! About to launch into a scathing attack on the abhorrent dishonesty perpetrated by the little thief, no matter to *which* temptations he had been subject, I was suddenly anticipated by a surprisingly sympathetic reaction from across the desk:

"Relax, Simpson," Mr Tod breathed softly: "for once, I'm on your side. To be perfectly honest, I think the man's got a bloody cheek."

"Well, thank goodness for that, Mr Tod. And what are you going to do about it?"

"But — as I was *about* to say — there's not a lot I can do. You *did* leave them unattended for a good twenty minutes, and if that gets out you're on a sticky wicket, son. I'm afraid he's got us by

130

the short and curlies, so I've arranged for a spot of parental liaison on Friday when I'll try to placate the wounded beast."

"But that's appalling, Mr Tod! What'll it mean to my classroom discipline if parents start dictating the conditions under which I can issue punishment exercises?"

"Nothing," concluded Mr Tod, "compared to what it'll mean to your GTC Registration if the self-important little prat starts broadcasting your abandonment of 1st Year Classes to the local press."

"But."

"Now if you don't mind, Simpson, I think I'll go and lie down in the sick room for a while."

Disbelieving, I watched his uneasy form huddle to the sick-bay, and made a mental resolution to call in at the Job Centre on my way home.

Thursday 23rd April

An evening party at a local hostelry to celebrate the long awaited arrival of back pay from our interim settlement.

Mr Pickup has even traded in his old Citreon car for a spanking new limousine from one of the Eastern-bloc countries and used tonight's celebration as an excuse for showing it off to the assembled company. He certainly seemed very proud and was confident that its initial steering problems could be ironed out before its first service was due.

In fact, several pints and three double whiskies later in the evening, he foolishly tried to convince a policeman that his collision with a lamp standard had been caused by the self same steering irregularity, but the officer seemed sceptical.

Sadly, the poor fellow was bundled unceremoniously into a Transit Van and, as I write, is understood to be 'helping with enquiries'; I trust we shall see him tomorrow.

Friday 24th April

The staffroom was abuzz with talk of Pickup's command performance last night: suggested reasons for his non-appearance this morning were many and varied, but I found myself preoccupied instead with minor celebrations over the business of Marshall. Mr Tod, having dragged a protesting and heavily-fevered body into school for the sole purpose of meeting Marshall Senior at Period 2, was somewhat irritated by the father's non-arrival. A telephone call to his home uncovered the revelation — from Mrs Marshall — that her husband had experienced a "night oan the bevvy" and that consequently he "wisnae fucked" about coming along to see the Depute after all.

There being little or nothing he could say in reply, Mr Tod — apparently determined to gain *some* degree of satisfaction from the affair — decided upon an individual interview with the boy himself, before calling for a taxi to ferry him home to bed.

Whatever he said during the discussion was certainly effective; to be honest, I suspect that Tod has developed some behaviour modification theories which owe more to threats of physical violence than to the effects of 'positive reinforcement', but a quivering and tear-stained Marshall had presented me with both the punishment *and* a written apology before the end of lunch-hour.

If only Mr Tod had been so helpful throughout the *rest* of my teaching career.

April — May 1986

A few months previous, the novelty of Mr Tod's more sympathetic approach might well have convinced Morris that a career in teaching was still a realistic proposition; the Depute's new-found altruism, however, made little difference at this stage, for mid-April had witnessed Morris following in the footsteps of so many teachers before and since — on his way to the Post Office, a second class envelope clenched firmly in his grasp, response to an advert intended to alter the course of his career.

It had been a hard task to sift through the multitudinous array of prospective jobs which offered the chance to earn "up to £20k in your first year", but it was always that "up to" phraseology which gave him cause for concern. Thoughts of joining the police, too, an extremely attractive option in terms of salary and career prospects, had had to be abandoned due to the chronic myopia from which he suffered. In short, Morris wasn't really fit for much else, but a *Guardian* advert tucked away inside an "Ethnic Community Rights" Special had chanced to catch his eye one Monday morning.

He hoped for an early reply; after all, he had enclosed a stamped addressed envelope without it being asked for, and he expected this courtesy to be noticed when his prospective employees began to sort through the lengthy list of applicants for the job. Meanwhile, educational economies bit deeper into the fabric of Parkland High, and Mr Ross's attempts to cut down on paper wastage in the photocopying room took on drastic proportions, as we shall discover.

The most noteworthy occurrence of these spring months, however, was undoubtedly the setting up of the long awaited enquiry into pay and conditions of Scottish teachers; chaired by Sir Peter Main, a former Chairman of Boots the Chemist, it was, of course, subject to a catalogue of headlines which hoped he would come up with "the right prescription" for the profession and it was, inevitably, bombarded with submissions from a host of interested parties throughout the subsequent months.

The *EIS*, for example, were first off the mark with a report which illustrated how increases ranging from 22.4% to 51%

would be necessary to equate their salaries with 1974 levels, and suggesting a 25% reduction in class sizes to accommodate the increased workload and changing nature of the job. Three weeks ahead of its own ambitiously tight deadline in producing the submission, the *EIS* intended to have the first words and — by using the next weeks to prepare answers to later submissions by other bodies — the last ones too.

Amongst these alternative submissions, the *SSTA* predictably enthused about larger pay differentials between primary and secondary teachers, the Government suggested that pay should almost certainly be linked to conditions of service, and the Scottish National Party chose to highlight — for reasons best known to itself — Central Region's *per capita* allocation of £13.50 per primary school pupil, a sum which they claimed "would not buy a dinner for two in an immemorable restaurant without the frills of a bottle of indifferent wine". Extending the culinary comparisons, the Lothian Parents' Action Group referred Sir Peter's committee to another group — that formed by an association entitled 'Philadelphia Women' — which had drawn American attention to the fact that it would be "a great day when our schools have all the resources they need and the Airforce has to hold a bakesale to buy a bomber . . . ". For Philadelphia, read Falkirk: education on the cheap, and on the backs of parental good-will, was not confined to Scotland alone.

The announcement of an independent review, however welcome, did not mean an automatic return to normality in schools: apart from the aforementioned continuation of curriculum boycotts, the *EIS* needed to ensure that a 'fighting fund' remained available for Session '86/'87, lest the Main Enquiry proved to have feet of clay and an equally stolid attitude to their demands. To Morris, it was a matter of little consequence, but there were some who had lost their stomach for the fight.

Monday 26th May

Bitterness abounds in the school, despite the encroaching conclusion to the session.

Half of Mr Pringle's union are still up in arms about having to pay levies for a strike they perceive as being over, while the other half are urging that contributions be *increased* to finance the expected escalation of action once the pay review recommends a 40-hour week and compulsory lunch-duties for all!

Personally, I'm glad to have demonstrated enough sense to remain in a moderate union, despite my frustrations over the future of education — at least I've saved myself a bundle of cash in levy contributions!

Mr Ross has been the subject of some fierce criticism as well. I *had* thought that Mr Pickup's description of our recently appointed Headmaster as "an interfering wee bugger" had referred to his initial insistence that we proceed apace with Standard Grade development after the interim pay award; in fact, it appears that general annoyance has been caused by the Head's refusal to countenance the large copper-plate inscription "Do Not Disturb At Intervals" on the Gents' Staffroom door. He claims that it makes our entrance hall resemble the outside of a honeymoon couple's bedroom door and has issued instructions for the offending banner to be removed forthwith.

Removed it may have been, but Pickup's replacement poster, comprising the stark command "GO AWAY" in six-inch black felt capitals was hardly likely to endear him to the Head's affections, and so it proved.

Personally, I feel that staff should be available for consultation at *all* times, and said as much to Pickup this afternoon, but he viewed my support for Mr Ross as symptomatic of the blatant sychophancy for which, he claims, I am renowned.

"Listen, Simpson!" he barked fiercely at me, "if there's one thing I can't stand, it's some snotty-nosed little brat coming to hand in a punishment exercise while *I'm* trying to get my feet up and my brain unravelled for the first time since breakfast. If they want us to work over the intervals as well they can start *paying* us over the intervals as well — and if that old fart," he motioned in the direction of the Head's study, "tells us to take *this* one down, then wait and see what goes up *next* time!"

I dread to think.

Tuesday 27th May

Pickup seemed in more jovial form this morning, despite the fact that he is still forced to utilise public transport to reach work, a state of affairs occasioned by the damage sustained to his car during an alcohol-induced collision with a lamp-standard after our pay-night celebrations last month.

Apparently, he has caught the 'Colditz Disease' too, for he had met Dickson last night, the fellow who left teaching last year to become a double glazing salesman, and his cheerful demeanour was not entirely unconnected with the fact that Dickson's firm is looking for new recruits. Although at the top of his earning scale in teaching, Pickup seems convinced that he will be able to double his salary at a stroke by following in the footsteps of our ex-colleague.

Sadly, he is probably right. Knowing of my *own* desire to leave the profession, of course, and noticing my attentive ears as he spoke of sales targets and bonus payments, Mr P. found it impossible to refrain from having some fun at my expense . . .

"And what about you, Simpson?" he crowed across the coffee table at afternoon break. "Why don't *you* get an application form?" he enquired archly, his voice laden with sarcasm. "Dickson tells me they're looking for high-fliers with just your credentials: y'know the kind of thing — individuals with flair, dynamic self starters . . . " he tailed off, unable to conceal a vulgar snort into his handkerchief.

For once, I found myself unwilling to turn the other cheek, and launched a somewhat underhand counter-attack.

"Yes, *I* do know the kind of thing," I replied tartly, " — and I also know the likelihood of getting a job like that when you're about to be prosecuted for being ninety milligrams above the legal limit! I doubt whether Dickson's boss is likely to drop the keys of a company Cavalier into *your* eager little lap!"

Silenced for once, the overbearing buffoon muttered something about 'turning worms' and retired behind his *Glasgow Herald* to lick the wounds I'd reopened so effectively.

Little did he realise that my interest in Dickson's job was purely academic: unbeknown to him — or anyone else — I've already secured an interview for a new job, and it takes place tomorrow!

Wednesday 28th May

Unfortunately, the secrecy surrounding my new job application collapsed when I entered the staffroom this morning.

"My God" exclaimed Mr Major — "Simpson's got a suit on! Where's the interview, sonny?"

My protestations that I merely felt like a change from the usual sports jacket met with a good deal of scepticism, and even my Registration class harboured few doubts about the reasons behind my unaccustomed sartorial elegance:

"Haw, check the new suit, surr!" bellowed Maclean as I entered the classroom. "Ur youse gaun for a new joab, surr? Urr ye? Eh?"

My categoric denials had little or no effect, but by 11am it didn't really matter: I was on my way to the Community Education Centre for the interview which was to change my life . . .

The job for which I'd applied was as a "Creative Play Leader", whose remit involved the organisation of a peripatetic team comprising YTS recruits who would visit socially disadvantaged areas to plan "creative play sessions" for a mixture of pre-school children and school phobics. Strangely enough, I'd seen the job in Pickup's *Guardian*, and had immediately felt that my experience in teaching, especially my enthusiasm for allowing the free and natural outpouring of expressive urges and talents, would make it an ideally-suited prospect.

I confess to momentary surprise at the apparent absence of any other interviewees, a surprise which turned to unease upon confronting the interviewing panel of three dungaree-clad, chain smoking, social workers.

Nevertheless, they all seemed tremendously pleasant, and I think they were impressed with my qualifications for the job: they certainly welcomed my liberal attitude towards the encouragement of child centred self-discipline, and they positively enthused over my intentions to encourage a greater proportion of community involvement from gay one-parent families in the scheme. But I hope the factor which may have swung the balance was my willingness to take the brightly coloured 'play-van' into areas of priority treatment and cater for the needs of ethnic minority children.

My own questions, at the end of the interview, were answered fairly and with candour.

"Funding of the scheme?" assured Eleanor, leader of the trio. "No problems, Mr Simpson — or can we call you Morris? The Manpower Services Commission should see us all right for the next couple of years, and once *it's* been disbanded we should be able to get the thing going again under the next quango the Government dreams up. If the MSC ever *were* to pull the carpet out, our usual practice is to abandon the whole caboodle and restart under a different name a few weeks afterwards. No, no, Morris — you needn't have any worries on that score. This'll keep you in beer money for quite a long time to come."

I wonder if that means I'm to be offered the post?

Thursday 29th May

No word until tomorrow about the results of my interview but — fingers crossed — I think I made a hit with Eleanor!

Employment prospects tended to preoccupy my thoughts for most of the day, though I was frustrated by further problems over the Xerox machine this afternoon . . .

Attempts to duplicate a set of creative writing stimuli for the 1st Year were confounded by the absence of the machine's feeder tray. Further enquiries of Mrs Thomson in the school office revealed that the Headmaster has locked the damned thing in his rolltop desk as a means of ensuring that all staff adhere to his draconian economy measures regarding copying-paper.

I told her that I'd never heard such ridiculous nonsense and informed her of my intention to confront Mr Ross immediately.

"You'll have a job," she smiled triumphantly across her typewriter, " — he's not back from the Rotary lunch yet."

"Not back from the — but it's nearly 3 o'clock!" I strained in disbelief.

"Sorry, Mr Simpson, but it's not my fault. You *know* Thursday's a bad day to see him in the afternoon, and I'm afraid he's the only one with access to the feeder tray at present. To be perfectly honest," she added unnecessarily, "it's a great relief for the office staff, and I can't say I'm unhappy to — "

"Thank-you, Mrs Thomson," I enunciated slowly in an effort to quell the wretched woman's impertinence. "That will be all."

Sadly, the dignity of my exit was marred by the necessity to clamber over several boxes of newly requisitioned duplicating paper which had been frustratingly piled at the office door.

The irony of it all.

Friday 30th May

Celebrations! The job's mine!

A telephone call at Period One assured me that a letter has been posted to confirm the appointment but that I could now consider myself, to all intents and purposes, in charge of the District's Play-Team.

Unable to keep the news to myself, I whispered the glad tidings in Mr Major's confidential ear at morning break, with the result that the entire school had heard of my success by mid-day! Major has restrained my initial impulse to tell the Headmaster what he could do with his job until I receive an official letter of appointment . . .

For the moment, I am sorry to report that Pickup's plans for leaving the profession as well have been dealt a severe blow by his lawyer's advice to plead guilty and get off with a twelve month driving ban; his geniality of earlier days has been consequently forgotten, and a pall of gloom had settled on his brow by afternoon break.

By 4 o'clock, his misanthropic tendencies had even extended to initiating a scurrilous rumour that I had been the only applicant for my new post; worse still, from his own point of view, the Head's latest injunction forbidding *all* notices which discouraged pupils from seeking staff attention has been met with the erection of a 12 inch high proclamation bearing the legend "BUGGER OFF . . . " in bold and stark lettering on the gents' staffroom door.

I don't think Pickup's doing his promotion prospects any good at all.

For my own part, I have rashly agreed to join a 'Booze Cruise' being organised by the Staff Social Committee for the last week of term. My natural aversion to such unprofessional antics was momentarily overcome by the euphoria surrounding my successful 'escape', and, I admit, by Miss Honeypot's coy suggestion that I "let my hair down for once".

I concurred, but have made it very plain that I shall stick to fruit juice all evening.

June 1986

Few people would have had the foresight, in August 1984, to suggest that Morris Simpson would have left teaching by the end of his probationary period. Yet, by the end of June 1986, that was what was to happen.

At least his departure would allow an extra statistic to be added to the shrinking total of vacant permanent posts which was held in his Region's staffing department: six weeks subsequent to his resignation, figures were released which revealed that 396 secondary teachers had been produced by Strathclyde colleges of education, yet only 130 posts were available; the position was worse for primary graduates, for whom there were only 18 jobs — and a grand total of 276 teachers waiting to fill them!

Diminishing school rolls, the difficulty of locating alternative employment and the increasing numbers of teaching mothers who returned to work as soon as possible after giving birth ensured that jobs were becoming scarce, and alternative strategies had to be devised in many emptying schools to ensure that teacher-time was being effectively used. The rationalisation of school resources demanded by falling rolls, for example, had already caused general upheaval, most particularly in the consortium arrangements which had been implemented over the preceding two years. On an equally innovative note, many secondary teachers found themselves retraining to be of use in other school departments: Jim Henderson, the Classics Department at Parkland, discovered that Mr Tod had tired of his "creative timetabling arrangements" and had put Jim's name down for a course leading to qualification in teaching Computer Education, an imposition he railed strongly against, but to no avail.

Some teachers, however, positively jumped at the chance to escape from the rigours of school life by attending college-based in-service courses during the school week. It was certainly an idea which appealed to Mr Pickup, should his hopes of entering salesmanship prove unfulfilled.

For Morris, though, none of it mattered any more, for he looked ahead to a new life, untrammelled by the bitterness

141

teaching. In many respects, it is a sad indictment of what had happened to the education system that he felt compelled to leave: there was a degree of truth in Mr Tod's assessment of our young hero as "a right banana", but Morris at least had a genuine desire to teach, a real affection for most of his pupils, and a healthy love of his subject. There were many like him, in the school sessions 1984 to 1986, who did not stand upon the order of their going, but vamoosed, as quickly and as painlessly as possible. There would be more to follow . . . .

For no matter the eventual outcome of the Main Enquiry, there were few people who believed that Scottish schools would ever be the same again. Much of the damage sustained in the two years of dispute was irreparable. We do not talk here of lessons taught, of examinations sat, or jotters marked. We talk instead of the indefinable qualities which go towards good teaching, and good education: impossible to sum up, or to categorise, they have something to do with a healthy and enthusiastic attitude towards school life in its manifold variations: the school parties, the after-school clubs and teams, the informal gatherings of pupils and staff outwith the strictures of classroom contact, moments when general attitudes to society, to education, to life, could be marked, chewed over, and inwardly digested — the "hidden curriculum", if you like.

Even allowing for the prospect of an eventual settlement — by no means guaranteed when Morris was due to leave, anyway — it had come as a salutory lesson to many teachers that so much of their previous enthusiasm seemed unnecessary: the world did *not* collapse, they had discovered, if you didn't take jotters home at night; the school kept running, they had realised, even if you *didn't* do lunch-duty; life stayed much the same if you didn't take the football team on a Saturday for some unpaid overtime, or organise a Sunday afternoon trip to the country. And yet the loss of such goodwill, such altruism, such enjoyment for the fullness of educational experience is incalculable. The likely disappearance of this non-contractual time may well be the most damaging legacy of the government of the day's repeated refusals to attempt a just settlement of the dispute before it became too late.

Eventually, one hopes, such an assessment might be found wanting, and the sense of vocation present within most teachers will come, alive and kicking, to the fore; by the end of Session '85/'86, some would have described that as a forlorn hope.

An examination of Morris's final diary for the *TESS* will reveal that, Main enquiry or not, there was still much dissatisfaction in secondary schools, Parkland High in particular. Unfortunately, for the lucky few who *did* get jobs in an increasingly competitive market place, there was never a guarantee that their time was going to be used effectively: jobs were usually on a temporary basis for the first months — or years —and were frequently as a replacement "supply teacher" to cover for absent staff.

Monday 23rd June

The final week of my two-year probationary period, a week which happily coincides with my departure from teaching within the secondary sector. My job in community education begins in the new session, and much clearing of desks will be required in the next five days.

Ironically enough, today saw the arrival of a *new* probationer in the school: Raymond McPhee is here "on supply" because of Miss Honeypot's enforced maternity leave which began last Friday, and I confess to a degree of surprise upon learning that the staffing department had sent a history graduate to replace a female P.E. teacher, but Mr Major assured me that this was in line with normal practice.

"Oh yes, Simpson," he affirmed over a post-prandial glass of wine this afternoon: "I'd be very surprised if he gets any PE classes to teach anyway — or History, for that matter. The usual thing is to allocate the 'sup' to any child-minding duties which might arise. You'll probably find he's at the top of Tod's 'please-take' list each and every morning."

"But that's ridiculous!" I spluttered. "The boy'll never get the chance to gain proper teaching experience *that* way. What on earth are they *thinking* about along at staffing?"

"Ours is not to question why, old son," the assistant head calmed. "The ways of God might be strange, but the ways of staffing are a damned sight stranger, as I think you'll agree if you have a wee chat with young McPhee when you get the chance."

Intrigued by Major's comments, I took the opportunity to

winkle Raymond out at afternoon break, and was alarmed to find the information verified:

"Oh yes, that's about right," he sighed resignedly. "This is my fourth temporary post since leaving college last August, and I've yet to teach three consecutive lessons to the same class. Anyway, thay say I'm getting near the top of the list now, and there may well be a permanent post by Christmas. With any luck," he added sarcastically, "it might even be a History one."

"But that's terrible," I consoled the fellow. "Surely it makes a mockery of your probationary report?"

"Well, I've certainly got a comprehensive spread of Headmasters' Assessments on it," he laughed, " — though I don't think I've made a very good start with *this* one," he motioned in the direction of Mr Ross's study.

Further explanations revealed that the headmaster had tried to give Raymond his usual Rectorial Address about the nobility of the teaching profession he was about to enter, as well as enumerating the manifold doors of opportunity which were about to be opened unto him; unfortunately, our newest recruit had been unable to conceal the snort of derisive laughter which had manifested itself upon hearing the Head's ridiculous assertions.

Raymond seems to know how many buttons make six . . . .

Tuesday 24th June

Mr Pickup, envious of my impending escape, has nevertheless had to abandon his own plans for leaving the profession. Predictably enough, his application for a post in double-glazing salesmanship — complete with company car — was rejected when his potential employers learned of his 12 month ban for drunken driving. Nothing daunted, however, he has announced his intentions of retraining as a teacher of Religious Education!

My incredulous reaction to the news was met with buoyant enthusiasm . . .

"Oh yes, Simpson," he chortled boyishly. "R.E.'s where it's happening, you know: a sabbatical year to retrain, and it's back to student days — two lectures a day, a couple of essays a month, and piss off home at two o'clock; not to mention," he winked slyly at me, "the young dolly birds in the students' union . . . "

Only too aware of the murky thoughts which lurked behind his leering smile, I attempted to divert the channels of conversation. "But what about your *prospects*, Mr Pickup?" I queried. "Surely there's no future in Religious Education?"

"On the contrary, my boy," he boomed, "since the S.E.D. decided to fall within the bounds of their own legal declarations, it's been the biggest boom area since the Guidance scramble of the 70's.

"Look at me! Geography promotion channels have been constipated for the past ten years, and look likely to be constipated for the *next* ten. By retraining in a *shortage* subject — if I can get past the queue of Classics Teachers trying to get in on it — I should get a P.T.'s post within three months of completing the course — and a nice fat chunk of responsibility cash to go with it!" he cheered, slapping me between the shoulder blades and marching off down the corridor, a definite swing in his step.

Perhaps he's right, but somehow I never imagined Pickup as a teacher of Religious Education, let alone a person fit to be granted an allowance for *any* kind of responsibility . . .

Wednesday 25th June

Much 4 pm comment in the staffroom over Raymond McPhee's resignation!

Apparently, the boy had been assigned to watching over the careers talks being given by the local constabulary as part of Mr Tod's pastoral care scheme. Notwithstanding his protests that the members of staff who were supposed to be teaching these classes should be there as well, instead of sipping tea and knitting pullovers in the staff common-room, he had nevertheless been forced to endure four sittings of a glossy presentation entitled 'A Caring Career — With A Future'.

His patience and disciplinary control had been understandably stretched to breaking point by Eliot of the 5th Year, who had punctuated the elderly sergeant's tape/slide presentation with a succession of increasingly audible grunts, comments about 'dirty pigs', and a rather obscene joke about a police horse and a truncheon.

Anyway, the upshot of Sergeant Black's little homily was

disappointing in terms of pupil recruitment, but young McPhee, having had ample time to mull over the possibilities of an alternative career in the police force, had eventually buttonholed the sergeant with a few pointed questions about salary, overtime, and special mortgage facilities, after which enquiries his name was added to the graduate recruitment list before anyone had time to say *Z Cars*!

The old order changeth, indeed.

Thursday 26th June

A booze Cruise this evening.

In an a moment of unguarded euphoria surrounding my successful escape from teaching last month, I rashly agreed to join this ocean-going venture, organised by the staff social committee.

Sadly, my illusions of a pleasant cruise along the shores of the Firth in a vessel of substantial and seaworthy proportions were shattered as the school mini-bus disgorged its contents of laughing and joking teachers on to the pier. Cries of "Where's the liner, then?" were met with a scruffily attired seaman leading us to the jetty-end, where our transport for the evening — a ship which bore more than passing resemblance to *The Vital Spark* — lay bobbing on the increasingly swelling seas some 30 feet below.

Foreboding in my heart, I tagged on to the end of a queue to the 'lower-deck gangways' and passed an order for fresh orange and lemonade to Pickup, who had organised a bar kitty for the evening.

Sad to relate, my last clear recollection is of viewing the receding pier with more than a tinge of apprehension as our diesel engines coughed a smoky trail across the bay; immediately thereafter, Pickup arrived with my drink, and the rest of the evening is a hazed memory. Not for the first time, I was suspicious of my colleagues' liberality in buying so many orange juices for me, but enquiries about spiked drinks met with wide-eyed innocence from all and sundry, just as before.

Suffice to say that my ensuing attacks of nausea and vomiting *could* be explained away by the twelve foot waves we encountered once outwith the shelter of the bay; not so, however, my repeated and persistent propositions to the headmaster's wife that she "come below deck for a quickie", which could hardly be attributed to seasickness.

I gather Mr Ross was singularly unamused, and can only hope he has already posted my final probationary report.

Friday 27th June

The last day of term — and my last day of teaching.

Of course, the school prize-giving has had to be cancelled due to intransigence by the Educational Institute of Scotland, and with only 65 pupils in attendance out of a school roll of twelve hundred, the day seemed somewhat flat and insipid, enlightened only by the interval presentations to staff members who were leaving. For my own part, I was anticipating the purchase of some crystal glasses with the money thereby gained, and looked forward to mentioning the fact to the generous donors.

Mr Ross, sadly, found himself unable to be present at the ceremony to wish me well, but Mr Tod made a lengthy and glowing speech wherein he seemed to suggest that community education's loss was his school's gain, though I think he got a little confused over the fact that I was *leaving* the latter to *go* to the former. Anyway, he spoke at such great length that my own carefully prepared speech was severely curtailed by the interval bell, so I had only time to mutter some brief words of gratitude for the staff's monetary gift.

This was probably just as well, for Pickup informs me that my missing speech was last seen forming the tail-section of a paper aeroplane squadron sent overboard last night. Indeed, the few words of thanks I *did* muster were practically drowned out by the whispered chantings of Pringle, Major and Pickup, in a strained and quavering version of "What Shall We Do With A Drunken Sailor?"

It all seemed so far removed from my bright expectations or those halcyon days at the beginning when, eager to fulfil my vocation, I entered the portals of secondary education. Frustrated by educational silliness and encroaching cynicism, however, I find myself desperate to leave while there's still a chance, and can only salute Raymond McPhee's initiative to stop before he'd really started!

To cap it all, Pickup tells me it's traditional to reciprocate the staff's generosity with bottles of whisky and sherry, as well as boxes of chocolates, for each staffroom. Unsurprisingly, the total bill for such a display of gratitude far exceeded the disappointingly meagre sum contained in my 'going-away cheque', and thus I find myself dispirited, frustrated, careworn — and severely out of pocket!

In a sense, I suppose that's what teaching's all about . . . .